LEGALIZED GAMBLING:

America's Bad Bet

by
John Eidsmoe

Resource *Publications*

An imprint of *Wipf and Stock Publishers*
150 West Broadway • Eugene OR 97401

Resource *Publications*
an imprint of Wipf and Stock Publishers
150 West Broadway
Eugene, Oregon 97401

Legalized Gambling
America's Bad Bet
By Eidsmoe, John
©1994 Eidsmoe, John
ISBN: 1-57910-568-8
Publication date: January, 2001
Previously published by Huntington House, 1994.

Contents

Chapter One

Could This Be Your Town?   7

Chapter Two

Gambling: The Lessons of History   23

Chapter Three

Gambling and Morality   37

Chapter Four

Gambling and Poverty   49

Chapter Five

Gambling and Economics   **59**

Chapter Six

Gambling and Addiction   **79**

Chapter Seven

Gambling and Crime   **93**

Chapter Eight

Gambling and Cruelty to Animals   **115**

Chapter Nine

A Winnable War:
We *Can* Defeat Gambling!   **121**

Appendix

Preachers and Politics:
What Does the IRS Allow?   **141**

Chapter One

Could This Be Your Town?

Phenix City, Alabama, 1954: a time and place of heroes, victims, and villains. That was the year Albert Patterson, a sixty-year-old Phenix City lawyer, resolved to run for attorney general of Alabama. His campaign crusade was to clean up the gambling syndicate that ran Phenix City, described by *Life Magazine* as the "wickedest city in the United States, . . . everything from gambling to murder to arson to fraud."

On June 1, Patterson beat the machine and won the Democratic primary. Eighteen days later, he lay dead on the streets of Phenix City—the victim of an assassin's bullet.

But, Patterson was victorious. The wave of moral outrage that swept Alabama and the nation after this brutal murder turned the tide and sounded the death knell for the gambling interests of Phenix City.

Phenix City's degeneration into "Sin City, U.S.A.," the assassination, and the subsequent clean-up by the judiciary and the Alabama National Guard under martial law, form one of the most dramatic chapters in the history of American justice.

Even in the 1800s, Phenix City was a curious mixture of aristocrats, fugitives, and convicts from British jails. For decades the city was known as a haven for bond-jumpers, rum-runners, and others involved in criminal activity. In 1918, when the army established Fort Benning in Georgia just across the Chattahoochee River from Phenix City, the gambling syndicate saw a golden opportunity to make a killing off young GIs and others willing to part with their money. Phenix City became known as "Little Las Vegas."

Casinos, lotteries, cockfighting, and other forms of gambling became big business in Phenix City, netting an estimated $100 million per year—not bad for a little town of about 23,000. Liquor, narcotics, prostitution, and other forms of crime became a way of life in Phenix City. The neon lights beckoned twenty-four hours a day, and, from 1945 to 1954, the town was the home of over one thousand prostitutes.

The fact that all of these activities were illegal in Alabama meant nothing. Phenix City had become a law unto itself.

Those who controlled gambling and other vices took control of the machinery of Phenix City government. The mayor, council, police chief, and county solicitor (prosecutor) were all controlled by the "machine." The sheriff was nothing but a "yes-man" for his chief deputy, Albert Fuller, a leading profiteer from the gambling interests. Fuller furnished legal protection to the brothels in exchange for one-third of the profits, and he forced many young women into prostitution by arresting them on trumped-up charges and arranging for the brothel operators to bail them out in exchange for "work." Despite his two-hundred-dollar per month salary as a deputy, Fuller loved to flash one thousand dollar bills and showered his many girlfriends with cars, clothes, and apartments.

Not everyone in Phenix City was corrupt. Like those of Las Vegas, the majority of citizens were decent and hardworking. Occasionally, crusading citizens tried to stand up to the machine; they were silenced by threats, beatings, and bombings, and some ended up in the Chattahoochee River. Most resigned themselves to the accepted order, rationalizing that since they didn't frequent the casinos and brothels, they weren't responsible or affected.

Phenix City also boasted more churches per capita than any other city in America—thirty-seven white churches and seventeen black churches, or one church for every 450 residents. Some churches opposed the gambling interests; others were controlled by them. Many of the gambling kingpins belonged to churches and contributed heavily. Ministers who opposed them were accused of mixing politics with religion and told to go read their prayer books. Frequently, they were transferred to other parishes, sometimes because of false allegations. Many were uncomfortable with the situation but didn't want to cause friction and jeopardize their churches, jobs, and families.

Reporters Edwin Strickland and Gene Wortsman tell of a layman, Hugh Bentley, who worked to galvanize the churches into action:

> It was in 1946 that Bentley took on the machine almost by himself. He was invited to speak before the Inter-City Club, composed of religious and civic groups, including the Phenix City Ministerial Alliance. The meeting was held at the Recreation Center.
>
> Bentley spoke on "Phenix City's Problems and Possible Solutions." Discussing the Lord's Prayer, he pointed out that Phenix City's problems were not so much economic, social, or political as they were moral.
>
> "I have maintained from the beginning," Bentley said, "that all this has been a religious matter. Until the people do something about the moral breakdown that allows gambling, unholy Sabbaths, and pros-

titution to operate openly, we will never make any progress because it isn't God's will."

At the end of his talk, Bentley was approached by the Reverend Paul Mathieson who asked him to give a similar speech at the Trinity Methodist Church on Laymen's Night. Bentley refused. He said the church was controlled almost entirely by Mayor Homer D. Cobb, head of the gangster-politburo for the city. But the Reverend Mathieson was insistent.

"Doctor," Bentley said, "I have a wife and three children. They'd burn my house down or kill me if I made that talk at your church."

"Are you a Christian, Mr. Bentley?"

"I try to be."

"If you are a Christian and if you refuse to suffer for Christ's sake, you are unworthy."

Bentley could not argue against that. He agreed to the talk but warned that both the minister and himself would pay for their actions. The speech was made as planned and as predicted Mayor Cobb called on the minister.

"Why was that talk allowed in my church?" Cobb said.

"It's not your church. It's the Lord's church," the minister replied. "The people needed the talk and should be told the truth."

"The people already know the truth," Cobb said. "I don't want such talks like that made in the future."

Of course there is no direct evidence that this led to the removal of the Reverend Mathieson, but when the next period occurred during which ministers could be reassigned, he was given a pulpit in another city. (Edwin Strickland and Gene Wortsman, *Phenix City* [Birmingham, AL: Vulcan Press, 1955], 181–2)

Bentley was not spared either. As he returned home the evening of 9 January 1952, he saw his home blown up with thirty-six sticks of dynamite. Fortunately, none of his family was seriously injured.

Soldiers from Fort Benning supplied much of the clientele even though commanders made most of the Phenix City establishments off limits to military personnel. Many a naive young soldier lost his paycheck at Phenix City, along with falling into vice, alcoholism, and drug addiction. Frequently, they were swindled by crooked operators; if they protested, well-armed bouncers beat them up and sent them back to Fort Benning battered, bruised, and penniless. In 1940, General George C. Patton threatened to send tanks into Phenix City to level Dillingham Street, the infested areas around Dillingham Street, and the Fourteenth Street Bridge. Secretary of War Henry L. Stimson called Phenix City "the wickedest city in the United States."[1]

Strickland and Wortsman say of Phenix City:

No practice was too vile. Unconsumed beer was re-bottled and re-sold. Drinks were spiked. Customers were knocked on the head and their wallets lifted. House men would take all the coin a soldier had, at a crooked dice table, then direct the youth next door to a company-owned pawnshop where he could pick up a spot of cash for his boots, his watch, or his underwear. Inevitably the boy returned to the table to lose again. If a client got rowdy, the casino tough would toss him outside, usually into the waiting arms of the police who would book him for being drunk and disorderly.

The Chattahoochee River became a dumping ground for dead bodies, the kind with cement-encased feet. Killings went unsolved. Complaints from honest citizens went unheeded.

You'd have to search a long time to find a home with green grass growing in the front yard. Dirt roads could be located by a turn of the head. The city jail smelled like the garbage dump and the county jail smelled like the city jail. (Strickland and Wortsman, *Phenix City*, 6)

This was the slime-pit Albert Patterson promised to clean up when he ran for attorney general in 1954. Two nights before the assassination, Patterson and his ally Howard Pennington pledged to each other that if one was killed, the other would work to bring the murderers to justice. One day before the assassination, Patterson told a church group his chances of taking office as attorney general were less than one hundred to one—an ominous prediction considering that, in Alabama in 1954, winning the Democratic nomination was almost tantamount to being elected.

On the night of July 18, Patterson worked late in his office. Then,

> at 9 P.M., he picked up his cane, which he used because of a World War I leg injury, and clumped slowly down the stairs to the street. His figure was outlined briefly under a street light as he turned the corner of the building to where his car was parked in an alley. Several persons, entering or leaving two nearby restaurants and a movie house, recognized the town's most prominent citizen.
>
> A moment later four pistol shots crashed in rapid succession, and the crippled crimefighter staggered from his car. For the first time since 1918 he walked without his cane. He walked fifteen steps with a bullet in his brain and two more in his chest before he fell, face-down on the pavement, at the bottom of the stairs leading to his office.
>
> He tried to speak to a youth who rushed to him. He strangled on his own blood and died without identifying his killer. (Strickland and Wortsman, *Phenix City*, 11)

News of the killing swept like wildfire through Alabama, and an aroused citizenry demanded action. But, law enforcement dragged its feet in the investigation.

As events unfolded, several heroes emerged. The first was John Patterson, son of the slain attorney general nominee. Vowing that he would smash the mob that had killed his father, Patterson announced his candidacy for attorney general in his father's place, charging angrily that the two men conducting the investigation, Russell County Solicitor Arch Ferrell and Deputy Sheriff Albert Fuller, were the most likely suspects. Patterson was elected attorney general and later served as governor. Today, at age seventy-two, he remains a judge on the Alabama Court of Criminal Appeals and is one of the state's most respected elder statesmen.

The second was Bernard Sykes. Attorney General Silas Garrett was controlled by the syndicate and was a bitter foe of Patterson. But, on June 23 he left the state for extended hospitalization in a Galveston, Texas mental institution, and Sykes became acting attorney general. Sykes promptly removed Ferrell from any further involvement with the case and took an active role in the investigation and prosecution himself.

The third was Major General Walter J. (Crack) Hanna, commander of the Alabama National Guard. The governor had ordered the Guard into Phenix City the morning after the shooting. General Hanna quickly became convinced Phenix City officials were performing a cover-up, but he had little power to do anything until July 22 when the governor proclaimed limited martial law. General Hanna and his guardsmen promptly disarmed the sheriffs and policemen and took over the administration of law in Phenix City. Their assistance in the investigation was invaluable.

The fourth was Judge Walter Burgwyn Jones, assigned by the Supreme Court to preside as special judge over the Phenix City proceedings. The sixty-six-year-old Jones had a distinguished history in Alabama. As a Confederate Major (later Colonel), his father Thomas Goode Jones carried General Robert E. Lee's flag of truce to General Grant at Appomatox and later served as governor of Alabama, a primary author of Alabama's 1901 Constitution, author of the Alabama Lawyer's Code of Ethics, which became the principal draft of the Code of Professional Responsibility of the American Bar Association, and a U.S. District Court judge.

Walter Jones himself had a distinguished career. In addition to being a judge, he served as president of the Alabama Bar Association, president of the Alabama Bible Society, editor of the *Alabama Bible Society Quarterly*, and author of some forty-five books on legal, historical, and biblical subjects. He taught an open-air Sunday Bible class that was attended by over one thousand men, and he founded the Thomas Goode Jones School of Law, which currently has over four hundred students and which, according to its statement of purpose and philosophy, is "dedicated to the fundamental concept that the rule of law is the foundation of our nation and that Biblical truth is the foundation of just law."

Judge Jones was a firm believer in the American Constitution. In his weekly newspaper column he declared that

> what we need in this country, for the good of all our people, is less centralized government, less extension of federal power and more local government. When the power of government is centralized in a government far removed from the people, and necessarily unfamiliar and uninterested with local problems, you do not have good government. . . .
>
> If the United States were to go along with the communist nations of the world to please them we'd lose all the freedoms we have. The communists are opposed to every great principle upon which our government is founded. They challenge all we hold dear and precious. We not only weaken our own nation, but we also weaken and let down the smaller nations of the world which are struggling to keep their freedom and their independence if we give any comfort to the communists. If we people in this country have even a thimble full of sense left, we will not change the form of our government one bit, we will not give up one single principle embedded in our Constitution and put there through blood and toil and sacrifice. The only way to deal with communism is to fight it every time and everywhere it rears its ugly head—

hit it with the biggest club available and
keep on hitting it until the world is secure
for people who want to be free sons of
God and not slaves. . . . (Walter B.
Jones, "Off the Bench," *Montgomery Advertiser* [11
July 1955])

A large man and an avid horseman with an
impeccable reputation for firmness and integ-
rity, Judge Jones seemed the ideal person to
take charge of Phenix City and restore order
and justice.

On 30 June 1954, flanked by guardsmen,
Judge Jones opened court. The Russell County
courtroom was packed with hostile mobsters,
racketeers, brothel operators, prostitutes, and
the like, as well as citizens hoping for a return
to law and order. As a military bailiff called the
court to order, Judge Jones delivered a prepared address:

> It is the unalterable determination of the
> State, of the Governor, and the people,
> that there shall be no return here of orga-
> nized crime and commercialized vice; no
> further continuance of a wicked regime
> which, for years, has burdened the county
> with an arrogant violation of the laws of
> God and man. There will be no return of
> the miserable days when a few gained
> wealth by holding in contempt the laws of
> the State, and by pandering to the lusts
> and base desires of men and women. . . .
>
> What is going on in this county today is
> not just a passing phase, not just a condi-

tion which will exist only for a few weeks or a few months—it is a permanent condition: all the powers of hell won't be able to prevail against it. . . .

I bring to the good people of Russell County the assurance of the Governor of Alabama that the State will do everything in its power to bring to an end the rotten situation here so long disturbing to the law-abiding people of the county. No longer is this county to be under the control and dominion of racketeers and gamblers and purveyors of prostitution.

Their insolent sway here forever ended on the night of June 18, when a cowardly assassin took the life of Albert L. Patterson and made his name the symbol of resistance to organized crime.

Albert L. Patterson rests in the earth from which he came, but the State of Alabama, all her forces of law, will not rest, day or night, until his murderer is tracked down and pays the extreme penalty for the brutal deed.

Let it be understood here and now, once and for all, that there will be no return to Russell County of that tragic era, the days when the law violator reigned supreme, and trampled the Constitution and laws under his foot. From this day forward the reign of law has come to Russell County to stay, and stay it will under the providence of God and all the power of Alabama's government. . . .

To those who have had part in the lawless-
ness in this county, who have made crime
their livelihood, who have grown fat in the
debauchery of our youth and the destruction of the morale of our Nation's young
soldiers, your day is ended, your hour of
reckoning is at hand, you stand at Arma-
geddon. . . .

It is not written in the book of fate, it is
not found in the pages of history, that crime
triumphs over law, that injustice prevails
over justice, and that evil grinds the good
in the dust. God's unchangeable laws do
not work that way, and they will not work
here. (Hon. Walter B. Jones, Presiding
Judge, comment from the bench at the
opening of the Special Session of the Circuit Court of Russell County, Phenix City,
Alabama, 30 June 1954, Thomas Goode
Jones School of Law, Montgomery, Alabama)

Judge Jones guided the grand jury with an
iron hand. As the nearby *Columbus (Georgia)
Ledger-Inquirer* editorialized,

Judge Jones is the recognized prophet of a
happier day in Russell County: Like the
Biblical prophets of old, he has joined the
fight against massive evil, and his words
are like mountain thunder rolling across
the sinful plain. Charging the grand jury
last week to examine Phenix City's ancient
iniquity, he said, "What a harvest of hell
and tragedy and crime it has bred! What
lifeless bodies it has helped put under the

ground! What human lives it has forever wrecked! What homes it has ruined!"

On another occasion he directed the jurors to "drive back into their lairs the beasts of crime," and declared that it would be better for "bats and owls to inhabit the city" than for vice lords to drain off the people's wealth. (Tom Sellers, "Judge Jones Heaps 'Fire and Brimstone' on Vice Elements in PC," *Columbus [Georgia] Ledger–Inquirer* [15 August 1954])

And the grand jury did their job. Over the next five months, they listened to voluminous testimony, evaluated evidence, deliberated upon charges, and returned 741 indictments against 144 defendants, including the leading figures of the syndicate. Of these, all but two either pleaded guilty or were found guilty.

Three men were indicted for the murder of Albert Patterson. The first, Chief Deputy Albert Fuller, was convicted of murder and sentenced to life imprisonment. He served ten years and was paroled and died in 1969 at the age of fifty, claiming his innocence to the end.

The second, Solicitor Arch Ferrell, was acquitted. The third, Attorney General Silas Garrett, remained in a mental institution in Galveston, Texas. The state of Alabama finally dropped the case against him in 1967.

Today, Phenix City is a quiet town of about twenty-seven thousand, with few signs of its sordid past. But, a generation has passed, and the lessons of history have started to fade. Alabama now allows dog racing, and certain forces in Alabama seek the legalization of horse racing, casinos, and lotteries as well. Governor Jim Folsom, Jr.—the son of Governor "Big Jim" Folsom supported by the Phenix City machine in 1954—has threatened to call for a special legislative session to consider, among other things, casino gambling.

Amid this controversy, Phenix City still stands on the banks of the Chattahoochee River as a grim reminder: After seeing what gambling does to a community, who in his right mind would vote for its return?

Endnotes

1. Edwin Strickland and Gene Wortsman, *Phenix City* (Birmingham, Alabama: Vulcan Press, 1955), 199.

Chapter Two

Gambling: The Lessons of History

"What's all the fuss?" gambling proponents ask. "Gambling has been around since the beginning of history. In fact, gambling is as American as apple pie."

Yes, gambling does have a place in history. As Jordan Lorence writes:

> Lotteries trace back to the earliest days of American history. The Jamestown colony in Virginia received financing from a 1612 lottery. The Continental Congress authorized a lottery to help finance the Revolutionary War in 1776. Early American colleges, such as Harvard, Yale, Brown, Columbia, Dartmouth, Dickinson, Rutgers, St.

23

Johns, Union, William & Mary, Yale, the Universities of Delaware, Maryland and Pennsylvania all obtained funding from lotteries. . . .

During the early 1800's, lotteries raised money for education and public works projects. (Jordan Lorence, *The Proposed Minnesota* Lottery [St. Paul: The Berean League of Minnesota, 1984], 2)

All of this is true. In fact, gambling traces its roots much further back than America's beginnings. According to William S. Garmon:

Games of chance are but the sportive survivals of a more serious practice—the art of divination. In the case of the spinning of the coconut or the blunted arrowhead, used in the art of divination to discover thieves, the transfer to the game of chance was quite simple. The Samoans, for example, ceased to use the coconut spin for its original purpose and came to use it for a game of forfeits and the casting of lots. The primitives came to recognize that much of life around them could be explained in terms of the laws of cause and effect. They were convinced that forces (gods) which had helped them in the serious enterprises of life would not desert them in a game.

Extant historical artifacts indicate that games of chance and gambling paraphernalia date back into antiquity. The western world and well over half of the nonwestern world are and have been highly addicted to gambling. In ancient China, Japan, Egypt,

Persia, Palestine, Greece, Rome, Java, and the Americas, indications of gambling are found. For example, bone dice were in use by the time of Homer [eighth century B.C.]. Knucklebones with numbers on four sides are found in Egyptian excavations dating to the eighteenth dynasty, in Indian ruins in the southwestern United States, and in the later ruins of Pompeii. In England dice-playing dates back to the Roman occupation. The Ice Age had hardly disappeared when crude dice were being used in southern France. A gaming board which was found on Crete dates to 1800 or 1650 B.C.

In the city of Rome gaming tables were discovered in the corridors of the Colosseum. Emperors Augustus, Caligula, Claudius, Nero, and Domitian were passionate devotees of gambling. A Hittite treatise written about 2000 B.C. discussed the feeding and training of race horses. The forerunner of the pinball machine is traced to the ancient Greeks who played a game using stones on a hillside. The Roman street loafers probably played a numbers game paying off on the number of soldiers who came through the gate at dusk. Paton points out that gambling seems to have had its chief hold where the race existed primarily in hunting, pastoral, military, or mercantile type cultures. The peasants who had to work hard for a living were comparatively free from the habit.

Since 1654, when Chevalier de Mere sought the help of Pascal in solving some of his

difficulties in dividing the gains from dice
games, mathematicians have given much
study to the theory of probability. If history teaches anything, however, it is that
people will continue to gamble, even
though they are made aware that the odds
against them are extremely high.

Gambling threaded its way into the vary
warp and woof of American life. It came
early, although this was hardly necessary
since the Indians the white settlers drove
out were avid gamblers. (William S.
Garmon, "Early Beginnings," in *The Gambling Menace*, ed. Ross Coggins [Nashville:
Broadman, 1966], 11–12)

We should add that Israel seemed relatively
free from gambling and regarded the gambling
practices of her neighbors as part of their idola-
trous worship of the gods of Fortune and Fate.
While Jesus Christ was being crucified, Roman
soldiers gambled for His robe (Matt. 27:35),
but the Jews did not approve this practice.

Garmon adds, concerning the lottery:

The lottery was first conducted at Roman
parties as a form of amusement for the
guests. Free tickets were given to each guest,
and later in the evening gifts were distributed to each ticket holder. The first money
lottery was held in Florence in the year
1530. By 1569, it had spread to England,
being used by the government as a means
of raising money. The rules of drawing were
as in Roman times. Each ticket holder received a prize. The lottery proved to be

very popular, and it was hailed as a painless form of taxation.

Most early American lotteries were of the Dutch type, with one winning ticket on the average to every four drawn, and were operated honestly by private enterprise. . . . They became an integral part of public financing in the colonies, being used by municipalities, churches, public utilities, development companies, and educational institutions. The First Baptist Church of Providence, Rhode Island, erected a building in 1775 with the proceeds of a lottery. The colleges of Harvard, Yale, Dartmouth, and Columbia (Kings) all used lotteries at one point in their history. . . .

In the year 1832, sixty-six million dollars was spent on lottery tickets in eight states. This was five times the Federal budget for that year. (Garmon, "Early Beginnings," 12–13)

Other forms of gambling flourished in early America as well. To again quote Garmon:

While one wing of the migrating gamblers worked up the Atlantic Coast and inland, another pushed from New Orleans up the Mississippi and Ohio rivers, forming great concentrations in cities like Vicksburg, Memphis, St. Joseph, St. Louis, Kansas City, and Chicago. The card, dice, and banking games, such as faro, craps, and poker, that became so popular in the United States, were all of foreign origin. According to Asbury, faro was the most popular game in the country during the nineteenth century. It was the nucleus upon which the elaborate gaming houses were built. It was also the first game to allow the introduction of extensive cheating which bred a horde of unprincipled sharpers.

When card games were introduced to America is not known, but it is thought that poker came through New Orleans. It was being extensively played in that city by 1825. The game of craps was also popular by this time, particularly with the lower classes. Card games were fast, and the period of uncertainty between the roll of the dice and the turning of the cards was relatively brief. The outcome of the game was soon known and frequent repetition was possible. This is probably the reason these games became popular in the gambling houses. Some of the other games of importance which enjoyed popularity were: roulette, pitch, monte, keno, three-card monte, hearts, chuck-a-luck, Boston, casino, and whist. The slot machine, which became a favorite in many areas, was not invented until the late nineteenth century. The pinball machine came into its own in the 1930s.

The legendary riverboat gamblers were the most fabulously dressed men of the era. Immediately prior to the Civil War fortunes were lost to these unprincipled sharpers as they plied their trade on the riverboats and in the ports of call. The professionals who followed the nation westward were not as flashy and are generally credited with more character. The standards on the frontier were rough, particularly in the mining towns, and a gambler's success depended on three items: chance, skill, and a fast draw. Many of these men became the leading citizens in the frontier communities. (Garmon, "Early Beginnings," 14–15)

All of this, it must be conceded, appears to be true. Gambling did occupy a prominent place in American history. The colonial experience, coupled with the riverboat gambling of the 1830s on the Mississippi and the casinos and poker games of the frontier, are indelibly impressed upon our consciousness.

But, this is only part of the story. Before we concede that gambling is a good, wholesome American tradition, we should ask: If gambling was such a respectable early American practice, why was it made illegal in every state by the 1890s?

The plain answer is gambling proved to be a national disaster! It resulted in all sorts of social evils, so around 1830 good citizens went to work for its abolition. New York and Massachusetts banned lotteries in 1833, and other states in the East followed shortly thereafter. By 1840, twelve states, mostly in New England, had outlawed lotteries. Gambling continued in the West into the latter half of the 1800s. But, by 1878, only one holdout remained, Louisiana, in which lotteries remained legal until 1893.

When the Louisiana legislature outlawed lotteries in 1892, the Louisiana lottery moved to Honduras, but, in 1895, Congress banned the sale of lottery tickets in interstate commerce. By 1900, legal lotteries had ended in the United States, as had other forms of legalized gambling.

Why the move to end gambling in America? Was it simply narrow-minded fundamentalist fanatics breaking up saloons and overturning gambling tables because they disapproved of anyone having fun? Hardly. In 1883, the United States Justice Department issued a study titled *Memoranda Concerning the Rise and Decline of the Lottery System in the United States*. It reads in part:

> A faithful account of the rise, progress and decline of the lottery system in the United States will furnish a melancholy chapter in the history of the American people. Few of the present generation [Note: this is being written in 1883!] have any adequate conception of the hold upon social and commercial institutions which the lotteries obtained in the first 30 years of this century, of the rapid growth of the gambling spirit engendered by them, of the vast evils resulting from them, which overspread the country, or of that widely extended movement against them, among moral and thoughtful citizens, which culminated, before the end of the half century, in their total suppression in many States and partial suppression in others. (United States

Department of Justice, *Memoranda Concerning the Rise and Decline of the Lottery System*, 1883)

On at least three occasions, the U.S. Supreme Court addressed the issue of gambling. In *Phalen v. Virginia*, 49 U.S. (8 How.) 163 at 168 (1850), the Supreme Court said,

> [E]xperience has shown that the common forms of gambling are comparatively innocuous when placed in contrast with the widespread pestilence of lotteries. The former are confined to a few persons and places, but the latter infests the whole community; it enters every dwelling; it reaches every class; it preys upon the hard earnings of the poor, and plunders the ignorant and simple.

The Supreme Court expressed similar sentiments in *Stone v. Mississippi*, 101 U.S. 814 at 821 (1879):

> They [lotteries] are a species of gambling, and wrong in their influences. They disturb the checks and balances of a well-ordered community. Society built on such a foundation would almost of necessity bring forth a population of speculators and gamblers, living on the expectation of what, by "casting of lots, or by lot, chance or otherwise," might be "awarded" to them from the accumulation of others. Certainly, the right to suppress them [lotteries] is governmental, to be exercised at all times by those in power at their discretion.

And, again in 1903 the Supreme Court upheld the power of Congress to prohibit the sale of lottery tickets in interstate commerce in *Champion v. Ames*, 188 U.S. 321:

> As a state may, for the purpose of guarding the morals of its own people, forbid all sales of lottery tickets within its limits, so Congress, for the purpose of guarding the people of the United States against the "widespread pestilence of lotteries" and to protect the commerce which concerns all the states, may prohibit the carrying of lottery tickets from one state to another. In legislating upon the subject of the traffic in lottery tickets, as carried on through interstate commerce, Congress only supplemented the action of those states—perhaps all of them—which, for the protection of the public morals, prohibited the drawing of lottery tickets, within their respective limits. It said, in effect, that it would not permit the declared policy of the states, which sought to protect their people against the mischiefs of the lottery business, to be overthrown or disregarded by the agency of interstate commerce.

Garmon explains some of the social problems associated with gambling in that era:

> Many evils, however, grew up with the lotteries. Since the lottery offices need to keep their employees busy in times other than when a lottery was being promoted, they started "little goes" on the side. These were primarily sucker traps, feeding on the poor

and servant classes. The greater evil, however, was "insurance" or policy. Essentially, insurance permitted an individual to wager for or against a certain number's being drawn on a certain day. The number could be bet to win, to lose, or to be drawn within a specified time period. Parlays and combinations were available. As the system grew in size it became profitable to attempt rigging the lottery. After repeated attempts to curb insurance failed, many governing bodies required that all lottery draws be completed in one day. (Garmon, "Early Beginnings," 13)

So, that's the full story. America experimented with legalized gambling early in its history. The experiment proved to be a disastrous failure, resulting in widespread corruption and exploitation of the poor. Americans learned from their mistake. A movement arose to abolish gambling, and, by 1900, most forms of gambling were illegal in all fifty states.

But, how soon people forget. As America moved into the latter half of the twentieth century, the moral values of earlier generations began to weaken. As the demand for government services continued to expand at every level, states began to look for additional sources of revenue, and the gambling interests gallantly offered to come to the rescue.

Nevada was somewhat different. Gambling flourished in Nevada in the 1850s, but citizens demanded an end to it, and, under territorial

Governor James Warren, Nevada adopted an anti-gambling law in 1861. The law was not well enforced, and, in 1869, Nevada legalized some forms of gambling with strict licensing requirements despite Governor Henry Blasdel's belief that "the bill is a blot and a stain upon the State of Nevada" (Craig A. Zendzian, *Who Pays? Casino Gambling, Hidden Interests, and Organized Crime* [New York: Harrow and Heston, 1993], 18). In 1909, Governor Denver Dickenson signed into law an anti-gambling law, and gambling was prohibited in Nevada until the legislature legalized it in 1931. In the 1940s, the big casinos came into operation. People thought of Las Vegas as an alluring place to go for an exotic weekend but not the type of atmosphere they'd want in their own home towns.

But, the neon lights of Las Vegas burned in people's hearts. Particularly in times of economic recession, thoughts of profit and tax revenue attracted many.

Lacking a sales tax and an income tax, New Hampshire legalized the lottery in 1964, and many other states followed. In 1976, Atlantic City sought to become the "Las Vegas of the East." Casinos, riverboats, racetracks, and other forms of gambling followed closely behind.

George Santayana said, "We learn from history, but we learn nothing from history." Perhaps, it would be more accurate to say that the lessons of history, learned so well by Americans in the late 1800s, have begun to wear off as memories fade.

America appears to be on the verge of a new wave of gambling mania; it is a hot issue in almost every state today. And, the consequences promise to be every bit as disastrous as before.

Chapter Three

Gambling and Morality

Throughout history the Church has led the fight against gambling. Augustine (A.D. 354–430) declared that dice were the Devil's invention, and, for nearly two thousand years, the various church bodies have been more united in their opposition to gambling than on most other social issues including abortion, alcohol, and tobacco.

And, the opposition was not limited to the Church. While gambling existed in early America, leading American Founding Fathers such as George Washington and Benjamin Franklin spoke against it; and, by the beginning of this century, almost everyone in respectable American society regarded gambling as a personal vice and a social evil.

Today, however, gambling has respectable defenders, even within the Church. "What's wrong with gambling?" they ask. "It's good clean fun, it doesn't hurt anybody, it brings jobs and revenue, and some people get rich!" The opposition is then caricatured as blue-nosed fundamentalists who are dead set on running other people's lives and imposing their own narrow-minded morality on everyone else.

To dispel this myth, those who oppose gambling must be able to give clear, cogent reasons for their opposition.

Harmful Effects

As later chapters will demonstrate, gambling has many harmful effects: creation of poverty, family breakup, gambling addiction, crime and corruption, spread of drugs and other vices, cruelty to animals, and others. These harmful consequences are themselves sufficient reason to oppose gambling.

But, even if gambling had no such effects, solid reasons exist to believe gambling in and of itself is immoral activity. Let's look at some of these reasons.

You Win at Others' Expense

Traditionally in America, and indeed in every market economy, one gains wealth by producing or selling something others want: goods, services, time, or capital. The greater the value of what you produce and sell, the more wealth you obtain in return. The best way to become rich is to produce and sell something others want and need.

And, in a typical transaction, both parties gain. Each party to the transaction values what he has received more than what he gave for it.

For example, I sold a quarter horse last year for nine hundred dollars. Why would I do that? I myself prefer to ride my faster Arabian, and the quarter horse was simply too large and strong for my young daughter, who really needed a pony instead. So, I decided that, for me, nine hundred dollars was of greater value than that quarter horse.

But, the buyer saw it differently. He is a cattleman, and he saw the horse's size, strength, appearance, and bloodlines and knew the horse could serve him well cutting cattle. To him, the quarter horse was of greater value than the nine hundred dollars. So, we made our exchange, and we each got what we wanted: I got the nine hundred dollars, and he got the horse.

And, if he can train that horse and make him a good cutting horse, and then sell the horse for two thousand dollars, that's great! He will have taken a raw material and made a more valuable finished product out of it, and, by increasing the value of the product, he deserves to profit. That's the American way of gaining wealth!

That's how exchanges take place every day in America. A restaurant buys one dollar of food products, invests time and labor into them, and makes them into an $8.95 meal. A hungry customer decides he'd rather have that meal than the $8.95 in his pocket; the restaurant owner decides to part with the meal because he wants the customer's $8.95.

It's that way with every transaction. On the job, you sell your employer eight hours of your time for seven dollars per hour. As a lawyer, you sell your time for perhaps one hundred dollars per hour, of which 50 percent is overhead. That's the American way of gaining wealth—selling others what they need and want.

But, in gambling, you win only to the extent that others lose. If you win a dollar at blackjack, it's only because someone else (another customer, or the casino) lost a dollar. If you win a million dollars on the lottery, it's because a million other people lost a dollar. You've given nothing of value for what you've won.

This road to riches is hardly a healthy philosophy of wealth. It leads people to think they don't have to give anything of value in order to find success. And, it provides no basis for pride of accomplishment or pride of workmanship.

Gambling Encourages Greed, Materialism, and Discontent

> And he [Jesus] said unto them, Take heed, and beware of covetousness: for a man's

life consisteth not in the abundance of the things which he possesseth. (Luke 12:15)

He that loveth silver shall not be satisfied with silver; nor he that loveth abundance with increase: this is also vanity. (Eccles. 5:10)

Let your conversation be without covetousness; and be content with such things as ye have: for he hath said, I will never leave thee, nor forsake thee. (Heb. 13:5)

But they that will be rich fall into temptation and a snare, and into many foolish and hurtful lusts, which drown men in destruction and perdition. For the love of money is the root of all evil: which while some coveted after, they have erred from the faith, and pierced themselves through with many sorrows. (I Tim. 6:9–10)

If riches increase, set not your heart upon them. (Ps. 62:10b)

Too often, opponents cite these passages as clear proof that the Bible condemns gambling. But, the passages need to be applied carefully. They do not condemn money per se, only an inordinate love of money, or greed. Other things besides gambling could lead to an inordinate love of money. And, theoretically at least, one could gamble without being greedy or loving money too much.

But, gambling, especially if it becomes addictive (see chapter 6), can lead to an obsession with money. In such instances, it leads to moral corruption and distorted priorities.

Gambling Encourages
Get-Rich-Quick Thinking

The 30 January 1994 *Montgomery Advertiser* describes a forty-three–year-old Florida man who

> earns $16,500 a year as an air conditioning installer in Florida and at the time was well on his way to racking up more than $17,000 in credit card debt.

> Nevertheless, he bought [a] shiny black Trans Am for $24,330, signing on the dotted line for a $22,783 loan from Barnett Bank of Pasco County. . . .

> "I was going to try to make the [$411-per-month] payments, but my money just didn't go far enough and there was no way I could do it," he said. "I flipped a coin about whether to buy it or not. It came up heads, so I figured maybe a miracle would happen—like winning Fantasy Five or the Lotto."

> The miracle didn't materialize. [The man], who never made the first payment, filed for bankruptcy in December. He says he expects to give the car back to the bank next month. (Helen Huntley, "Many Americans Won't Face Up to Financial Problems," *Montgomery Advertiser* [30 January 1994]: 13F)

Examples like this abound. Where gambling is widespread, some people daydream about winning big through gambling rather than working hard, saving, and investing. Often their daydreams remain exactly that—daydreams—and they remain poor and unproductive. Or, they may act on their dreams and overspend, and, when they find themselves in hot water financially, they head to the casino or the racetrack to bail themselves out—and usually just get themselves further in debt.

And, when, on very rare occasions, they do win big, they tend to spend their money foolishly because they don't appreciate it as they would if they had earned it. So, all too soon, they are poor again.

Solomon recognized this fact of life nearly three thousand years ago:

> He that tilleth his land shall have plenty of bread: but he that followeth after vain persons [RSV: worthless pursuits] shall have poverty enough. A faithful man shall abound with blessings: but he that maketh haste to be rich shall not be innocent. (Prov. 28:19-20)

> Wealth from gambling quickly disappears; wealth from hard work grows. (Prov. 13:11, Living Bible)

Gambling Is Poor Stewardship

If our money were simply our own and no one else's, then gambling might merely be foolish. But, when we remember that ultimately all things belong to God and that we are stewards of the resources He has given us, then gambling becomes poor stewardship of His resources. As Matthew 25:14–30 tells us, our Lord will hold us accountable for how we use His resources.

Gambling also takes on moral significance when we remember that we are responsible to provide for our families: "But if any provide not for his own, and specifically for those of his own house, he hath denied the faith, and is worse than an infidel" (I Tim. 5:8). If, because of gambling, we are unable to provide our spouses and children with the food, housing, clothing, education, and other things they need, then gambling clearly has become a moral issue.

Morality and Legislation

The gambling interests' trump card is "Regardless of how you feel about the morality of gambling, you can't legislate morality." That's a bogus argument if there ever was one. All law consists of moral judgments based upon ultimate values. A law against murder constitutes a value judgment that murder is wrong because man is created in the image of God—and we don't hesitate to impose this value judgment upon those who disagree. A law against stealing is a value judgment about who has a right to property and the wrongfulness of theft. Law makes value judgments every day.

Second, regardless of the morality of gambling itself, the many social evils associated with gambling—poverty, addiction, organized crime, etc.—make gambling a proper subject for legislation.

Third, gambling proponents in many cases seek much more than just legalized gambling by individuals. In many instances, particularly involving lotteries, they seek to enshrine gambling as a state-run institution. Casinos and racetracks usually are not run by the state, but they are heavily regulated, protected by the police, eagerly promoted by state tourism bureaus, looked upon as sources of revenue, often afforded monopoly status, and treated almost as public utilities. If you can't legislate morality, how about legislating immorality?

Gambling vs. Speculation

But, some will ask, is gambling really any different from investing in the stock market or in commodities or futures or in real estate?

First, high risk investments of this nature might be morally wrong if we invest more than we can afford to lose or if our investment losses prevent us from meeting our legitimate financial obligations.

But, speculation is not the same as gambling. The speculator/investor does not simply play a numbers game and trust blind chance. He studies the market carefully and makes only those investments that in his best judgment are likely to make a profit. He knows he could be wrong, so he risks only so much as he can afford to lose. And, he probably diversifies his investments, so if one goes bad, the others will sustain him.

And, the speculator/investor is not seeking something for nothing. Rather, he is putting his money to work, letting others "rent" his money while they use it for constructive purposes.

Suppose an investor has one hundred thousand dollars. If he buys General Motors (GM) stock, he is lending his money to GM. GM then uses that money for capital improvements, etc., and the investor realizes a profit as his GM stock increases in value.

Or, if the investor puts his money in a savings account at 4 percent interest, the bank puts his money to work by lending it to home builders, car buyers, business entrepreneurs, etc. The investor is not seeking something for nothing. Rather he is giving something of value—the use of his capital—in return for a profit.

Gambling Sees a World Governed by Chance, Not Divine Purpose

Unlike the laborer who honors the Divine command that "In the sweat of thy face shalt thou eat bread" (Gen. 3:19a) and the investor who tries to understand and apply the laws of economics, the gambler's worldview is that of a universe governed by blind chance or the luck of the draw—a random universe without order, purpose, direction, or design.

In fact, the pagan nations which surrounded Israel, such as the Babylonians, made a religion out of this chance, random worldview, and they deified and worshipped good luck and bad luck as gods. Isaiah warns, "But ye are they that forsake the Lord, that forget my holy mountain, that prepare a table for that troop [RSV:

Fortune], and that furnish the drink offering unto that number [RSV: Destiny]" (65:11).

Nolan P. Howington says concerning this passage of Scripture:

> The deities mentioned here, Fortune and Destiny (Gad and Meni) were the gods of fate, and were symbols of good and ill luck. The prophet's protest was against those Israelites who trusted to chance rather than God. It also involved those who sought a syncretized religion that included both the God of Israel and the gods of luck. The prophet's disclaimer contains an abiding insight: Faith magnifies the providential care of God; the cult of luck menaces such faith. Forms of activity that tip the hat to chance or preserve the worship of luck must therefore be seriously questioned by the religiously motivated individual. (Nolan P. Howington, "Biblical Insights," in *The Gambling Menace*, ed. Ross Coggins [Nashville: Broadman, 1966], 21)

Solid reasons do exist, then, for concluding that gambling is immoral:

1. It has harmful consequences for the individual, his family, and society.

2. In gambling, one wins only to the extent that others lose.

3. It involves greed, materialism, and discontent.

4. It causes get-rich-quick thinking that frequently leads to idleness, recklessness, and irresponsibility.

5. It involves poor stewardship of God's resources and often causes us to fail to provide for our families.

6. It is the opposite of sound investment planning.

7. It involves the worship of "Lady Luck" as a form of idolatry.

Now, can you suggest some good reasons why one *should* gamble?

Chapter Four

Gambling and
Poverty

My first exposure to gambling came at an early age. My parents and I moved from South Dakota to Sioux City when I was a child. Sioux City is located in northwest Iowa where three rivers come together; across the Missouri River is South Sioux City, Nebraska, and across the Big Sioux River is North Sioux City, South Dakota. Sioux City was a cattle town, with one of the largest stockyards in the world.

At that time, gambling was illegal in Iowa. But, one had only to cross the Missouri River for horse racing in Nebraska, or cross the Big Sioux River for dog racing in South Dakota.

49

I spent my high school summers working in a lumberyard by the stockyards. Ranchers from the cattle range country of western Nebraska and South Dakota would bring their livestock to the stockyard, and then we'd load their trucks with lumber, fenceposts, etc., for the trip home. Most of the men I worked with earned minimum wage or a little above. Many of them had large families to support. And, yet, every Friday night many of them cashed their paychecks and headed across the Missouri to bet on the "ponies" or across the Big Sioux to bet on the "puppies"—always with hopes of winning big.

Occasionally, they won a little; usually, they lost. And, throughout the week that followed I would hear them complain that their children didn't have milk, that their utilities were about to be cut off, that their bills couldn't be paid.

The link between gambling and poverty was thus indelibly impressed upon my mind. My observation was not unique. Many studies have concluded that the gambling industry preys especially upon the poor. And, since a disproportionate number of poor people gamble and the poor spend a disproportionate share of their income on gambling, an attempt to raise revenue by means of a tax upon gambling is a regressive tax.

Prior to opening his famous casino in Reno in 1946, Bill Harrah employed a research team to identify probable gamblers. The research revealed that the most likely clientele were low-income people.[1] He planned his casino accordingly, arranging bus service to bring customers from thirty-one cities, low-priced meals as enticements, etc.

The same seems to be true nationwide. The gambling industry aims primarily at low-income customers and elderly customers. The occasional wealthy "high roller" does exist, but he is the exception. The fact that about 50 percent of Nevada casinos' income comes from slot machines rather than the gambling tables, demonstrates that the "high rollers" are not the main source of income.[2] Those least likely to gamble appear to be middle-class Americans, although the gambling industry is now trying to break into this market.[3]

This is particularly true of lotteries. As the U.S. Congress noted in its 1976 study entitled *Gambling in America*, "The lottery is one of the more regressive forms of gambling—that is, people in the low income categories spend proportionately more on it than those in the higher income brackets."[4]

Charles T. Clotfelter and Philip J. Cook, professors of public policy studies and economics at Duke University, reported their findings in the *Journal of Economic Perspectives* in 1990:

> Lottery play falls with formal education. For example, a survey in California found that the proportion of adults who participated during one week in July 1986 ranged from 49 percent for those with less than a high school education to 30 percent for those with a college degree. With respect

to occupation, in the California survey lottery play was most common among laborers (including both skilled and unskilled) at 46 percent, and least among advanced professionals. Retired people and students played least of all. With respect to race, survey evidence suggests that Hispanics in the west and blacks in the east play more than non-Hispanic whites.

Remarkably, the same sources of data do not demonstrate any consistent relationship between lottery play and household income over the broad middle range; the average expenditure in dollars for households making $10,000 is about the same as for those making $60,000. One implication of this pattern of demand is that the tax implicit in lottery finance is regressive, in the sense that as a percentage of income, tax payments decline as income increases. (Charles T. Clotfelter and Philip J. Cook, "On the Economics of State Lotteries," *Journal of Economic Perspectives* vol. IV, no. 4 [Fall 1990]: 112)

A University of Michigan study also found that poor people spend a greater proportion of their income on gambling.[5]

"A 1982 study of New Jersey lottery players found residents of low-income minority neighborhoods playing the state's numbers game in a proportion more than half again as large as their share of the general population."[6] Another Illinois study revealed that the ten ZIP codes with the highest household incomes averaged per capita annual lottery sales of $76 while the ten ZIP codes with the lowest household incomes averaged annual per capita sales of $221.[7] Daniel B. Suits, professor of economics at Michigan State University, notes that low-income lottery players wager a disproportionately high percentage of their income on the lottery,[8] and Mark Abrahamson, professor of sociology at the University of Connecticut, reports that Connecticut's daily numbers game (a form of lottery) "primarily attracts poor, long-term unemployed and less educated participants."[9]

In 1979, a study of New Castle County, Delaware, revealed that there were no lottery outlets (places to buy tickets) in the upper-income neighborhoods where 17,630 persons lived, one outlet for every 17,774 persons in upper-middle income neighborhoods, one outlet for every 5,032 persons in lower-middle to middle income neighborhoods. and one outlet for every 1,981 persons in poor neighborhoods.[10] And, the *San Jose Mercury News* study reported that an "analysis of household income and lottery sales in 1,332 ZIP codes across the state [of California] shows that lottery sales in the poorest 20 percent of the zones was significantly higher than in any other zone for a period spanning October 1986 to March 1988." The study found that the average per person spending on the lottery among persons living in a household with a median household income range of $7,743–$18,751 was $116.94, while the average per person spending in households averaging $34,131–$75,001 was $53.42.[11]

The *Des Moines Register* reported that "a dollar from Iowa's poorest citizens is at least five times as likely to be spent on the lottery as a dollar in any other income group and . . . lottery players earning less than $10,000 play the lottery several times more often than higher-income groups."[12]

Even Daniel W. Bower, president of Scientific Games and a producer of lottery products and services, has acknowledged that the player selection or numbers game, a form of lottery, attracts low-income, minority players, typically with less than an eighth grade education.[13]

The gambling industry argues that casino gambling is less regressive than other forms and point to Nevada as an example. But, these Nevada statistics are misleading, for they are based on out-of-state customers at a time when Nevada was the only state in the West where casinos were legal, so, as Braidfoot observes,

> Residents of other states, especially those that did not border on Nevada, had to have sufficient resources to travel there. . . .
>
> When the survey focused on Nevada, where the game was legal and where players did not need to have a sum of money to travel there, casino gambling was very regressive. In fact, casino gambling in Nevada was more regressive than any legal form of gambling throughout the nation. (Larry Braidfoot, *Gambling: A Deadly Game* [Nashville: Broadman, 1985], 114)

Since gambling itself is regressive, taxation of gambling revenues is likewise regressive, in that the poor pay a greater share of their income to that form of taxation than do the rich.

Some argue the merits of a progressive income tax, claiming it is only fair that the rich should pay a greater portion of their income in taxes than should the poor. This is the principle upon which our progressive income tax is based. Others argue that the progressive income tax is unfair, that the rich and poor should pay an equal percentage of their income in taxes.

But, no one would argue that a regressive income tax, in which the poor pay a higher percentage of their income than the rich, is the fairest system of taxation.

No one, that is, except those who stand to benefit from a regressive business—like the gambling industry. So, what does gambling do for the poor? It preys upon them and makes them poorer. And, they and their families suffer as a result.

Fortunately, some refuse to go along with this racket. Recently, in an advertisement in a California newspaper, Holiday Quality Food Stores made the following announcement:

> Since the California state lottery program started, . . . we have sold in excess of $1 million worth of lottery tickets. Our food business during this same period has declined the same amount. Morally, we feel that it is wrong to offer our customers the opportunity to gamble with their food

dollars and therefore we will no longer be selling [lottery tickets]. ("News You Might Have Missed," *Editorial Resources* [March 1987]: 11)

Holiday Quality Food Stores, if I lived in California, you'd get my business!

Endnotes

1. *USA Today* (15 January 1986): B-1, B-2; see also Larry Braidfoot, *Gambling: A Deadly Game* (Nashville: Broadman, 1985), 112.

2. Iver Peterson, "While Atlantic City Rolls On, Las Vegas Comes Up Losing," *New York Times* (21 October 1984): 2E; *Venture* (June 1986): 103.

3. *USA Today* (15 January 1986): B-1, B-2.

4. Commission on the Review of the National Policy Toward Gambling, *Gambling in America*, 94th Cong., 2d sess., 1976, 1.

5. *Gambling and State Lotteries* (Marlborough, NH: Plymouth Rock Foundation, 1988), 3.

6. Robert K. Landers, "State Lotteries," *Editorial Research Reports* (27 February 1987): 98.

7. *Chicago Sun-Times* (27 March 1988).

8. Daniel B. Suits, "Gambling Taxes: Regressivity and Revenue Potential," *National Tax Journal*, vol. XXX, no. 1, (March 1977): 22–9; "Economic Background for Gambling Policy," *The Journal of Social Issues*, vol. XXXV, no. 3 (1979): 52–7; *The Christian Science Monitor* (12 May 1982): 10; "Gambling as a

Source of Income," in *Michigan's Fiscal and Economic Structure*, ed. Harvey E. Brazer (Ann Arbor: U of Mich Press, 1982), 828–853.

9. *Dallas Times Herald* (1 December 1977).

10. Delaware Council on Compulsive Gambling, *The Impact of State Sponsored Gambling on the Community* (1979).

11. *San Jose Mercury News* (1 May 1988).

12. *Des Moines Register* (24 August 1986).

13. Daniel W. Bower, "Video Lottery Devices: A New Generation of Players," *Fourth Annual Gaming Conference and International Gaming Congress* (Philadelphia: Laventhol & Horwath, 1982), 23–4.

Chapter Five

Gambling and Economics

Try this experiment with a friend (a good friend, so you don't get ripped off): Give your friend one hundred dollars, and he gives you one hundred dollars back. You've just completed an economic transaction. But, are either of you any richer as a result? This ridiculously simple illustration demonstrates a key point: A mere exchange of economic assets does not necessarily create wealth.

Government at all levels has increased dramatically in size. George Washington took office in 1789 with a total of 350 federal civilian employees; the total federal budget in 1832 was

$11 million. In 1994, the federal budget is
$1,400,000,000,000 (that's $1.4 trillion), with an
annual deficit in 1994 of $198 billion and a
total national debt of $4 trillion. State and local
government budgets have exploded as well. As
a result, all levels of government are searching
frantically for new sources of revenue. But, new
tax revenues are hard to find, especially in a
society of increasing expectations and sagging
economies.

Enter the gambling industry with the solution. "We're a real growth industry," they say.
"By 1995 Americans will spend $40,000,000,000
($40 billion) annually on gambling. Just let us
into your state, and we'll bring you jobs, tourists, tax revenues, and just exactly the economic
shot in the arm your state needs."

That $40 billion figure sounds tempting. But,
as Eugene Martin Christiansen, a leading gambling industry consultant, says:

> As America approaches the dawn of a new
> millennium, its industrial might withering,
> the business of chance prospers. The auto-
> mobile, steel and electronic industries are
> in shambles while legal gambling is one of
> the country's fastest-growing businesses,
> touted by the politicians as the way to re-
> vive dying towns and create jobs. . . .
>
> That casinos create no new wealth, that
> they act to take money from many people
> and funnel it to the few lucky enough to
> hold a casino license, seems of little conse-

quence to the growing number of politicians urging more gambling on the public. (Eugene Martin Christiansen, *The Sun Herald* [18 October 1992]: A-1)

Likewise, William R. Eadington, writing for the Bureau of Business and Economic Research, notes that casino gambling does not create wealth; it simply concentrates and re-allocates it.[1]

Real creation of wealth occurs when one creates a product or performs a service that is of value to others. The farmer who raises crops or livestock, the food processor who refines raw materials and packages them into food products, the trucker who transports them to a local community, the grocer who makes them available to you by displaying them on his shelves, all have a role in creating wealth, and they profit as a result. The same could be said of the landowner who raises timber, the logger who harvests it, the sawmill that refines it into lumber, the trucker who transports it, the lumberyard that sells it, the contractor who buys it and, together with his construction workers, builds a new house, have created a new article of wealth.

But, no new wealth is created in gambling. Money is simply transferred from one person to another. This does not benefit society; in fact, it may even be harmful. Let's look at the economic claims of the gambling industry and see whether they really have merit.

Attracting Jobs

Milton McGregor, a wealthy racetrack owner who is waging a political battle to bring casino gambling to Alabama, claims his gambling proposals would bring twenty-four thousand new jobs to Alabama. Ironically, he says this is needed to save Alabama's present racetracks from financial ruin. McGregor writes:

> The choice we must make is whether we will progress into the largest industry in our history, casino gambling, or will we stagnate and lose the existing industry that has operated successfully for 20 years. There is not middle ground.

> Tax revenues are behind drained from Alabama because 40 percent of the Mississippi casino's revenues are supplied by Alabama residents. This new competition will only be a two hour drive from Birmingham and only one hour from Greenetrack.

> Victoryland's handle is already down by 15 percent as a result of Mississippi casinos that are a four hour drive from Macon County. Our studies show that the casino in Philadelphia, MS. would cut into the Birmingham handle by 30 percent. We cannot stand that type of impact on our business and the taxpayers cannot afford to pay the higher taxes.

> This issue is not a luxury but a matter of survival. In order to be competitive we must have the same type of entertainment options that our competition enjoys. We must

have casinos, a lottery and horse racing. Florida has the lottery, horse racing and Jai Alai. Georgia now has the lottery and there is Indian gaming.

The question that every taxpayer in Alabama must decide is do you want to pay higher taxes and have fewer jobs, or would you prefer to have 24,000 new jobs and $150 million per year in tax revenue paid voluntarily by gaming patrons. I think the choice for us is clear. (Milton E. McGregor, "Alabama Will Get 24,000 New Jobs," *Economic Gazette*, vol. I, no. 1 [August 1993]: 5)

Consider for a moment, twenty years ago, when the greyhound racetracks came to Alabama, they simply wanted a license to operate. Let us operate, they said, and we'll bring jobs, revenue, and prosperity for all. Now, they tell us, they're going to go broke unless they can have casinos, lotteries, and horse racing as well. They need these in order to compete with Mississippi, Georgia, and Florida.

Be assured, the competition from other states isn't going to stand still. If we give Milton McGregor his casinos and lotteries today, what will he demand twenty years from now in order to stay competitive? Stripshows? Legalized prostitution? Still, McGregor's promise of five thousand new jobs is tempting. But, will it really happen?

Past experience indicates otherwise. As the Plymouth Rock Foundation reports:

Atlantic City, NJ, is an example of what gambling can do to a city and county. Gaming casinos there are legal. The city has become "Las Vegas of the East." It draws people from as far south as Washington and as far north as Boston. Atlantic City has one of the [highest] welfare rates in the U.S. Jobs were scarce in that seaside resort before the advent of gambling. With influx of casino workers, how was the job market? Unemployment is the same as it was before the casinos were opened. (Plymouth Rock Foundation, *Gambling and State Lotteries* [Marlborough, NH: 1988], 4)

And, yet, Atlantic City's casinos do employ many people. Why does the unemployment rate not improve?

One reason is that jobs created by the gambling industry merely take jobs away from other more productive sectors. As Robert Dildine, economist for the state of Minnesota, put it, "Money in an economy will be saved or spent. The multiplier works in either place. If the money is spent at the race track, the multiplier works there, and it will stop working at the grocery store or ball park where the money used to be spent."[2] In other words, money spent gambling is money that would have been spent in other ways. If a person didn't have the option of betting at the horse track, he would spend his money at the football stadium or on other forms of entertainment or purchasing groceries and other things. Or, he would save

and invest his money, putting it to work to
benefit himself and others. Money spent gambling just means less money spent or invested
elsewhere. Jobs created by gambling just mean
less jobs elsewhere. Dr. Walter Heller, professor of economics at the University of Minnesota and economic advisor to the Kennedy Administration, and Sung Won Son, senior vice-
president and chief economist for the Norwest
Banks, expressed similar sentiments; as Dr. Son
said, lotteries create no new wealth; they merely
shuffle economic resources from one part of
the economy to another.[3]

For example, when the lottery was introduced in Illinois, many retail businesses began
selling lottery tickets. But, Walgreen's, a major
drug store chain, found that ticket buyers
clogged the stores and bought nothing else.
Walgreen's stopped selling lottery tickets, and
other businesses did likewise.[4] At the same time,
gambling shifts money away from other businesses; when the casinos move into an area,
legitimate businesses are often forced to either
sell or close down. The 1994 Goodman study
reports that the number of restaurants in Atlantic City declined from 243 in 1977 (the year
after casinos were legalized) to 146 in 1987,
partly because the casinos advertised cheap
meals to lure customers inside.[5]

The Plymouth Rock Foundation concluded:

> As for higher employment and more busi-
> ness, records indicate employment and rev-
> enues may increase for businesses feeding

off gambling but dry up for other enterprises. And as for economic impact, opponents suggest many of the dollars gambled
away would have been spent on tangible
items and productive pursuits that could
have turned money over and over in the
market place, thus generating jobs and
taxes, etc. (Plymouth Rock Foundation,
Gambling, 3)

Second, the introduction of gambling into a
state or community usually results in an influx
of new people who absorb the jobs. After noting that the Atlantic City casinos had not generated as many new jobs as hoped, Eadington
notes:

Nevada's performance in total number of
jobs is somewhat more impressive. Closer
observation, however, indicates that the casino industry there attracts a highly mobile
and transient work force. Home ownership in Reno and Las Vegas ranked in the
lower 15 percentile of the nation. (William
R. Eadington, "The Casino Gambling Industry," cited in *Casino Gambling: Panacea
or Paradox?* [Mobile: Christian Life and
Public Affairs Committee of the Mobile
Baptist Assn., 22 December 1992], 15)

Local residents, in other words, did not
benefit from the casinos' job creation nearly as
much as they had hoped.

Third, gambling may retard job creation because it makes it difficult for a state to attract
new industry. As will be demonstrated later,

the social problems associated with gambling—alcohol, drugs, crime, financial instability, etc.—do not create a good work force within a state. The adequacy of the local labor force—particularly in terms of quality and reliability—is a key factor industries consider in determining whether to locate in a state. As Lycurgus Starkey observes, "Gambling hurts industry. Governor Sawyer admits it is difficult to attract new industry to Nevada because of the presence of gambling, the consequent fear of absenteeism and employee instability."[6]

When the gambling industry boasts of the number of jobs they expect to bring into a state, it is appropriate to ask how many jobs are eliminated or kept out of the state as a result.

Fourth, while the gambling industry brags of the number of people they employ, they usually say little about the types of jobs created or the wages paid. The *Wall Street Journal* recently noted that Atlantic City's casinos employed 41,473 people in 1991. But, most of these jobs paid only a little above minimum wage; the average card dealer earns only about five dollars per hour. Recently, a female investigator worked undercover for a Las Vegas casino as a "keno girl." She was paid only forty-five dollars for an eight hour shift ($5.63 per hour) and was repeatedly told to show more "breast" to the customers.[7]

Employees of the horse racing industry fare no better than those who work for the casinos. As Braidfoot says,

[In 1984 the] average jockey earned between eight and fifteen thousand dollars. How is that for precise statistics? But that amount, whatever it was, included a 25 percent commission which had to be taken out for the agent who arranged "mounts." Other expenses had to be deducted.

Over half of the jockeys (52 percent) in 1983 had a mount less than one hundred times during the years, or once every three to four days. The average purse money won by the horses ridden by these jockeys during an entire year was $7,194! One out of every five jockeys had only ten races for the entire year, with an average annual purse winning of $511! Twenty-nine percent of the jockeys did not win a single race!

Kellman states that 84 percent of the jockeys riding in New York, among the most lucrative racing circuits, do not even make a living wage. (Larry Braidfoot, *Gambling: A Deadly Game* [Nashville: Broadman, 1985], 83)

Those who raise racehorses are also included in the gambling industry's job creation statistics. But, a study in Michigan in 1982 revealed that the average thoroughbred operation employed 2.1 full-time laborers at an average annual salary of $8,000, and 2.4 part-time workers at an average annual salary of $1,470.[8]

One reason those who raise thoroughbreds pay their laborers so little is that despite a few multi-million dollar horses, the average person who raises thoroughbreds nets very little profit and often loses money. Many enter the business primarily as a tax write-off—hardly an argument that gambling generates tax revenue![9]

And, what of those who work at the racetracks? As an owner of horses myself, I appreciate the glamour and romance of horses, but I sometimes lose sight of the romance when it is time to clean the stables. Braidfoot reports:

> Many of these individuals live in dormitories located in the backstretch [the straight part of a race track opposite the part leading to the finish line]. Daily preparation and training activities begin before sunrise and conclude well after sunset. It is not unusual for work schedules to be eighteen hours a day, seven days a week, at a weekly salary of less than $200. (Joint Legislative Task Force to Study and Evaluate the Pari-Mutuel Racing and Breeding Industry in New York State, *Pari-Mutuel Horse Racing and Breeding in New York State: An Economic Profile* [1 April 1982]: 40)

These are the jobs the gambling industry brags they will bring to your state!

Attracting Revenue

In addition to twenty-four thousand new jobs, gambling mogul Milton McGregor boasts that legalized gambling would bring $150 million in new revenue to the state of Alabama. To legislators who are searching for ways to balance the budget and finance government programs and to citizens who are already over-taxed, this sounds tempting indeed.

But, would gambling really bring these new revenues to Alabama, or to your state? Let's analyze this claim.

First, these claims are based in part upon the gambling industry's promise to bring new jobs. If the jobs aren't created, most of the promised tax revenue will never materialize either.

As we have seen in the preceding section, the promise of new jobs is shaky to say the least. In many cases, they do not materialize; where they do, they often simply take jobs away from other industries. The fact that gambling enterprises and their employees are paying $150 million in taxes to your state, if true, does not mean your state has gained $150 million in additional revenue. It could just mean that the gambling industry has siphoned jobs and in-come away from other businesses that would have paid the same amount in tax.

Also, as previously noted, wages paid by the gambling businesses tend to be extremely low. The amount of taxes gambling employees would pay, if any, would be negligible.

Third, taxes paid by the gambling industry itself, as distinguished from the taxes paid by their employees, would be very regressive. As we have seen in chapter 4, low-income people spend a disproportionate amount of their in-come on gambling when compared to other socio-economic groups. A system of taxation in which the poor pay a greater percentage of their income than the rich is inherently unfair.

Fourth, increased tax revenues generated by the gambling industry are to a large extent offset by increased demand for government services for the racetracks and casinos—police and fire protection, safety inspections, road construction, etc. As Braidfoot reports concerning Atlantic City gambling revenue, "The net gain has been minimal."[10]

The lottery presents a unique situation because this normally does not involve taxation of the lottery industry, but rather the state actually running the lottery. Even so, the benefits are negligible.

First, the state makes money off the lottery only to the extent that the citizens lose. In any organized gambling industry, the odds are somewhat stacked in favor of the house; in the long run and by the law of averages the house must win more than it loses, or it can't stay in business. To whatever extent the lottery is a good deal to the state, to the same extent it is a bad deal for the people who play the lottery. This seems so simple and obvious that it hardly needs to be stated, but the point is often overlooked.

In fact, lotteries pay out in prizes only about 50 percent of the amount they take in.[11] For every $1 million customers spend buying lottery tickets, only about half a million will be returned in prizes.

Suppose someone were to propose a bet

with you: "Flip a coin; the odds of heads or tails are 50/50. If you win, I pay you one dollar; if I win, you pay me two dollars." Would you take that bet? Of course not, but that's essentially what the lottery does.

Does that mean all of the remainder is revenue? Hardly. As former *Atlantic Monthly* publisher James K. Glassman reports:

> The states actually own the game and promote it heavily, using vast public resources. California, for instances, spends $180 million on lottery administration and marketing; Minnesota, $60 million a year, or 19 percent of the total.
>
> To make matters worse, lotteries are an outrageous ripoff. State governments are involved in what can accurately be called a con game.
>
> In blackjack and roulette in Las Vegas, the house take (including taxes) is only a few percentage points; in horse racing, it's about 20 percent; in sports betting with a bookmaker, about 5 percent. Compare those figures with the state's take (including expenses) in a lottery game—about 50 percent. Compare those figures with the state's take (including expenses) in a lottery game—about 50 percent. In Iowa, for every $100 that's bet, just $24 gets returned to customers as prizes. (James K. Glassman, "Lotteries: Games Are Ripoffs, But Remain Popular," *Montgomery Advertiser* [26 December 1993]: 3K)

So, if about 50 percent is paid out in prizes and about 34 percent is revenue, what happens to the rest? Much of it goes to economic research and advertising; some of goes to bureaucracy; some (about 5 percent) is paid in sales commissions to those stores that sell lottery tickets.

You could say that about 16 percent of every one hundred dollars spent on lottery tickets is consumed by overhead. Or, put another way, you could say that for every one hundred dollars of net income from lotteries (gross sales minus prizes), about 32 percent is overhead. Either way you figure it, lotteries are an extremely inefficient way of raising revenue.

As a result, the revenue raised by gambling falls far short of expectations. The 1976 U.S. Congressional study, *Gambling in America*, concluded, "No state now derives more than 3 percent of its total revenue from lotteries, and it would be futile for state policy makers to look to lotteries as a substitute for traditional forms of taxation."[12] Jordan Lorence, however, notes that in 1982 the New Jersey lottery constituted about 4 percent of state revenues;[13] but, with Atlantic City, New Jersey is a unique situation.

According to the Christian Life Commission of the Southern Baptist Convention:

> In only three or four states does the income from gambling contribute more than 4 percent to a state's budget. In most states with legalized gambling, revenues from lot-

teries, off-track betting, and all other forms of gambling amount to less than 2 percent. Gambling produces nothing, and gambling adds nothing to the economy or to society. On the contrary, it is uniformly and consistently disruptive. (Christian Life Commission of the Southern Baptist Convention, *Issues and Answers: Gambling* [Nashville, TN], 3)

The gambling industry sometimes tries to entice the public by suggesting that gambling revenues be earmarked for special purposes like education, hospitals, etc. This is their way of buying respectability and of winning over constituencies like the education lobby.

But, in fact, this adds nothing to education or any other special fund. If $100 million of gambling revenues are earmarked for education, this just means the legislature will appropriate less money from the general fund.

Again, gambling creates no new wealth, and, therefore, gambling creates no new revenue. Money paid into the state coffers through gambling just means less money paid into the state coffers by other means.

While a brief book like this cannot fully answer the many pressing questions concerning state budgets, the solution has to be found in other ways: developing a sound and stable industrial and economic base, designing an adequate and equitable tax structure, and limiting the role of government to those functions which are essential.

Attracting Tourists

Gambling is necessary to attract tourists, the argument goes. Without casinos and racetracks, our hotels and convention centers will not be able to compete with neighboring states that offer these attractions. And, if we don't have casinos in Alabama, our citizens will just go across the border to Mississippi or Georgia or Florida, and spend their money there. There is some truth to this argument, but its validity is limited and counterbalanced.

While gambling may attract some kinds of tourists, it may also repel others. Would you take your children to Las Vegas or Atlantic City for a family vacation? Certainly, gambling attracts many respectable people, but it also attracts many other kinds. Is this really the kind of tourism your state wants to specialize in?

And, the more gambling proliferates, the less of an attraction it becomes. Las Vegas and Atlantic City lose much of their glitter and attraction if the same casinos are available in Philadelphia, Mississippi, or Grand Forks, North Dakota.

To keep attracting tourists when gambling is available at home, states must continually advertise more exotic forms of entertainment. What will those be? Better odds (and therefore less revenue)? Strippers? Prostitution? Complimentary cocktails? Drugs?

And, whatever benefits are realized by attracting tourism are more than offset by the economic drains of gambling, each of which will be discussed in detail in later chapters:

• Gambling addicts, the crimes they commit, and the cost of treating them.

• Alcoholism, prostitution, and other costly social problems that often accompany gambling.

• The introduction of organized crime.

• Economic factors such as increased poverty among many, divorce, bad credit, bankruptcy, welfare, time lost from work, etc.

Sometimes a society is faced with a difficult moral dilemma: Do what is right, or do what is profitable. Should we as a society promote or condone immoral activity even if it will benefit us economically?

If the choice comes down to that, I hope we as a society will do what is morally right. In the long run, this is far more important.

But, fortunately we are not faced with that kind of choice. Not only is gambling morally wrong; it is bad for the economy as well. This shouldn't be surprising. God's principles are not only right; they are also practical.

In the long run, the best way for a state or community to plan for economic growth is to concentrate upon the quality of life. Business and responsible productive people are likely to locate in a state or community if they are convinced that this is a good place to live and raise a family and if this community is made up of stable, productive, responsible people who will make good neighbors and good workers.

Economically, the ultimate question should be: Would legalized gambling make your state or your community a better place in which to live?

Endnotes

1. William R. Eadington, "Trends in the Legalization of Gambling in American in the 1980s and Implications for Australia," Bureau of Business and Economic Research, Paper No. 86-2.

2. Jordan Lorence, *The Proposed Minnesota Lottery* (St. Paul, MN: Berean League of Minnesota), 15.

3. Ibid., 15-16.

4. Ibid.

5. Robert Goodman, et. al., *Legalized Gambling as a Strategy for Economic Development*, United States Gambling Study, Center for Economic Development, University of Massachusetts, Amherst (March 1994): 54.

6. Lycurgus M. Starkey, Jr., *Money, Mania and Morals* (Nashville: Abingdon Press, 1964), 60.

7. Thomas F. Roeser, "Chicago Casino Plan Gambles City Future," *The Wall Street Journal* (12 August 1992): A-10.

8. Larry Braidfoot, *Gambling: A Deadly Game* (Nashville: Broadman, 1985), 84.

9. Ibid., 77-81.

10. Braidfoot, *Gambling*, 121.

11. Christian Life Commission of the Southern Baptist Convention "State Operated Lotteries" (Nashville, TN), 1; see also James K. Glassman, "Lotteries: Games Are Ripoffs, But Remain Popular," *Montgomery Advertiser* (26 December 1993): 3K.

12. Commission on the Review of the National Policy Toward Gambling *Gambling in America*, 94th Cong., 2d sess., 1976, 161.

13. Lorence, *Minnesota Lottery*, 9.

Chapter Six

Gambling and Addiction

The handsome young black lieutenant sat in my office as we talked. He had been convicted of bad check charges in a military court-martial, and my assignment as an Air Force Reserve Lt. Colonel was to perform a clemency evaluation—to interview him, examine the record, and determine whether the conviction and sentence were appropriate.

What would lead this intelligent, articulate, personable, capable, and motivated young officer to embark upon a course of action that would destroy a promising career? He had become a compulsive gambler, and he had written bad checks to support his gambling habit.

Nearly everyone knows about drug addiction and alcoholism. Most people know that drug addicts and alcoholics often are driven to commit crimes to support their habits. But, many people are unaware that a condition like compulsive gambling exists.

Perhaps that's because compulsive gambling is often whitewashed with such romantic euphemisms as "gambling fever" or the "spell of Lady Luck." In the American mind, the frontier gambler even holds a certain romantic aura or mystique.

But, compulsive gambling does exist, and it is recognized as a personality disorder by the American Psychiatric Association;[1] as such, compulsive gamblers are subject to medical and/or administrative discharge from the Air Force and other branches of the service. As stated in *The Gambling Menace*,

> As in the case of the alcoholic, the compulsive gambler is a sick person. An eminent doctor [Dr. Iago Galdson] holds that alcoholism, gambling, and superstition form a triad, because each has essentially the same causal factors. On the basis of clinical experience, he discovered that his parents carried into adulthood emotional and psychological dynamics that belong to the pre-adolescent and childhood periods.

> The psychodynamics of gambling are so deep-seated that psychiatrists are still searching for the roots of the problem. Sigmund

Freud relates the compulsion for gambling to the conflict over masturbation. The addiction for gambling becomes an unconscious substitute for masturbation and affords self-punishment for it. Ralph R. Greenson relates gambling to satisfaction for latent homosexual, oral-receptive drives, and gratification of unconscious needs for punishment. (Henlee H. Barnette, "Rehabilitation of the Gambler," in *The Gambling Menace*, ed. Ross Coggins [Nashville: Broadman Press, 1966], 97–98)

Mental health professionals attribute different reasons for compulsive gambling: escapism, addiction to ecstatic tension, grandiose delusions, sometimes a masochistic desire for self-punishment accompanied by a secret desire to lose and suffer defeat and humiliation.

Each compulsive gambler has his or her own story. Especially sad is that of Mary Warwick, described as

a shriveled, white-haired wisp of a woman, slumped in her wheelchair in front of the slot machines that jangled and whirred on the pink-and-purple carpet under the glittery chandeliers of the Trump Taj Mahal.

On her lap was a gray plastic trash bag filled with her belongings: a couple of sweaters, a roll of toilet paper, a few big plastic Bally's Park Place cups for her winnings. The cups were empty.

An hour earlier, Mary, 72, had picked up her $467 monthly disability check—her only money besides Social Security and food stamps—at the Atlantic City Rescue Mission, a crowded homeless shelter that she calls home.

More often, though, Mary lives at the casinos. That is where she spends hours and days on end, methodically jerking the handles of the Jungle and the Royal Flush and the other slot machines. She stops only to eat a little something, or to snooze for a few hours in her wheelchair, right there in the hubbub of the casino floor. She stays until she has gambled away her government checks or until, in her sleep, she falls out of her wheelchair and the guards pick her up.

She gambles, she says, because of a child long gone. "I hate gambling now," Mary said.

"I lost a lot of money, but I can't stop. It makes me feel unconscious. I can't feel anything. It makes me forget about my little boy. (Pam Belluck, "Homeless Gamblers Caught Between Casinos, Shelters," *Nashville Banner* [26 November 1992]: A-49)

And, compulsive gambling is much more widespread than most people realize. A new study, released March 1994, by Robert Goodman of the Center for Economic Development at the University of Massachusetts at Amherst, estimates that "up to 5 percent of the adult population and 8 percent of the teenage population have some form of problem or pathological gambling behavior."[2]

As gambling has become legalized, the number of compulsive gamblers has increased. In the last ten years, the number of compulsive gamblers has doubled, from four million to eight million[3]; other estimates give an even higher figure (Goodman's new figures would translate to 9.3 million adults and 1.3 million teenagers). Valerie Lorenz, executive director of the National Center for Pathological Gambling in Baltimore, says, "We are viewing compulsive gambling as the mental health epidemic of the 1990's."[4] Arnold Wexler of the Council of Compulsive Gambling in New Jersey says, "We're creating a nation of gamblers."[5]

While most problem gamblers are male, an increasing percentage are women. Wexler says women constitute about 25 percent of all compulsive gamblers.[6] And, children are not immune from the spell of gambling. Today, about 20 percent of those in attendance at meetings of Gamblers Anonymous are women, and about 20 percent are teenagers.[7] Over 90 percent of compulsive gamblers began gambling before they were twenty-one-years old.[8] Often being exposed to one "big win," either winning oneself or being around someone who has won, makes an indelible impression and leads to compulsive gambling. Seventy-two percent of Atlantic City High School students gamble in the casinos, according to the testimony of a specialist counselor.[9] Psychologist Durand Jacobs says teenagers frequently get into the casinos even though the legal age for admission is twenty-one; some even are given complimentary mixed drinks. Dr. Jacobs calls gambling "the growing addiction of the 1990's,"[10] and notes that 10 percent of teens who gamble are problem gamblers, as compared to 5 percent of adult gamblers.[11]

The same is true in Minnesota:

> Although gamblers must be 18 years or older to enter most Minnesota casinos, some teens boast about the ease with which their friends have been able to sneak past security guards.
>
> "Just go with a friend who's old enough, and walk in while he's showing his ID to the guard," said one teen who was playing blackjack—and losing—recently at Treasure Island Casino in Red Wing.
>
> And because gambling has all the properties kids love—instant gratification, blood-pumping excitement—some experts believe they're more liable to get into trouble once they start. (Pam Schmid, "Problem Gambling Rising Among Teens, Some Experts Say," *Montgomery Advertiser* [12 January 1994]: 2C)

The *Montgomery Advertiser* describes the experience of one college-age gambler:

> During his sophomore year, the same year he started supporting himself, live blackjack made its debut at the casino—and his habit spiraled out of control.
>
> "Now I'm thinking, 'I can turn $20 into

$100,'" he recalled. "It got to the point where I would take an entire paycheck with me and lose it and fall behind on rent."

There was no catching up. By the summer of 1992, he was broke and constantly lying to his parents. One fateful weekend, he decided to win some of it back during a road trip with friends. But he ended up losing so much money at a Hudson, Wis., dog track that his rent check and several others would have bounced if his parents hadn't bailed him out.

"Without their understanding and help, there's no way I would have survived," he said. (Schmid, "Problem Gambling," 2C)

The gambling industry itself is aware of this problem. As Braidfoot says, "A recent address at a thoroughbred racing meeting warned that widespread availability of lottery tickets in vending machines would make those tickets available to high school students. Students will be putting their lunch money into lottery tickets. Although the speaker's concern may have been more one of concern over competition than concern about the welfare of the children, he certainly was accurate about the facts."[12]

In fact, sometimes the gambling industry prepares children to become gamblers. The *Clarion-Ledger* notes that *The Biloxi Belle* in Biloxi, Mississippi, is preparing an arcade to entertain children while their parents gamble. The children are being prepared to become the next generation of gamblers.[13]

Gambling addiction is not limited to the casinos and racetracks. Psychologist Marvin Steinberg, who heads the Connecticut Council on Compulsive Gambling, says the legalization of lotteries in Connecticut has increased gambling addiction in that state and adds, there are compulsive gamblers who will say, "my thing was lotteries."[14] Msgr. Joseph Dunne, president of the National Council on Compulsive Gambling, says state promotion and advertising of lotteries makes the problem of compulsive gambling worse. He believes lotteries do create compulsive gamblers, especially the instant lottery that provides the fast action many compulsive gamblers want.[15] In fact, many who might never enter a casino or racetrack would nevertheless buy a lottery ticket at a convenience store and thereby become addicted. Modern technology makes it possible to bring the lottery right into the home, via the television and the computer modem. And, of course, one who is introduced to gambling through the lottery becomes much less resistant to other forms of gambling, and his lottery addiction can lead him to other forms of betting, just as softcore pornography can lead to hardcore, beer can lead to hard liquor, and marijuana can lead to hard drugs.

How does one recognize gambling addiction, either in oneself or in others? Psychiatrist Edmund Bergler offers the following characteristics of problem gamblers:

1. Gambling is a typical, chronic, and repetitive experience in his life.

2. Gambling absorbs all his other interests like a sponge.

3. The gambler is pathologically optimistic about winning and never "learns his lesson" when he loses.

4. The gambler cannot stop when he is winning.

5. No matter how great his initial caution, the true gambler eventually risks more than he can afford.

6. The gambler seeks and enjoys an enigmatic thrill which cannot be logically explained, since it is compounded of as much pain as pleasure. Thus, the title of gambler is reserved for a specific group of neurotics.[16]

Compulsive gambling hurts the individual, but it also affects society as a whole. As *Psychology Today* reports:

In terms of human damage, pathological gambling can be extremely destructive. Politzer [Psychologist Robert Politzer, who works with the Maryland state treatment center for compulsive gamblers] estimates that each compulsive gambler disrupts the lives of 10 to 17 others, including his relatives, creditors and co-workers. The economic price is also high. According to the [Maryland] center's findings, the average compulsive gambler usually bets twice what he makes, and costs society approximately $40,000 a year. (Dr. Robert Politzer, cited by Johnny Greene, "The Gambling Trap," *Psychology Today* [September 1982]: 55)

Gambling also is associated with family problems. One Connecticut study revealed that 10 percent of problem gamblers had been married three or more times, compared with 2 percent of the general public.[17]

Dr. Valerie Lorenz, head of the New Foundations program in Maryland, notes that 12 percent of the families treated at her clinic are now on welfare, with welfare's attendant social problems. She insists that tax revenues derived from legalized gambling must be weighed against the unemployment, bankruptcy, theft, and other social consequences of compulsive gambling.[18] As Congress noted in its *Gambling in America* study, "Deleterious effects on society include loss of funds by lending sources, loss of time from the job and associated costs, and the cost of imprisonment and providing support for families whose funds have been depleted."[19]

Still another cost is the debt accumulated by gamblers. Henry R. Lesieur, Chairman of the Department of Criminal Justice Studies at the University of Illinois at Normal, says the unpaid gambling-related debts of those in gambling treatment range from fifty-three thousand dollars to ninety-two thousand dollars. Many of these file bankruptcy, meaning their creditors probably never get paid.[20]

The cost of establishing and running treatment centers for compulsive gamblers must be considered as well. For if the state is going to promote gambling, the state arguably has a moral obligation to treat those who become gambling addicts.

And, a major cost is the crime committed by compulsive gamblers to support their habit. This cost is staggering and frightening, as we shall see in the next chapter.

But, in my view, an understanding of compulsive gambling is incomplete without a recognition that man is an inherently religious being. The reader will recall that Isaiah warns against those who forsake the Lord and instead prepare a table for Fortune and a drink offering for Destiny (65:11). As we saw in chapter 3, Fortune and Destiny (Gad and Meni) were the pagan gods of fate, the symbols of good and bad luck.

Compulsive gambling is, or can be, worship of those pagan gods. Aaron J. Rosanoff, in his *Manual of Psychiatry and Mental Hygiene*, calls the gambling impulse "mystic faith in luck."[21] Maurice Parmalee, in *Personality and Conduct*, calls the gambling impulse "a belief in personified luck."[22] *Look Magazine* senior editor Grereon Zimmermann simply says that "most gambling is an unreasoned primitive plea for Dame Fortune's favors."[23] One remembers the Broadway musical *Guys 'N Dolls* in which the gambler places all his hopes for love, marriage, and the future on a dice game, and, as he gets ready to roll the dice, he sings pleadingly, "Luck, Be a Lady Tonight."

Newsweek summarizes it well:

> The gambler's compulsion is triggered by the first big win. When inevitably, a losing streak sets in, the compulsive gambler increases his bets. As his losses become greater, superstition and magic began replacing the gambler's keen judgment. He uses up his earnings and falls behind in his debts. In time, the gambler's personality degenerates, his career and family life may be ruined and his life becomes a nightmare. (Diane Weathers, et. al., "Gamblers Who Can't Quit," *Newsweek* [3 March 1980]: 70)

Why do some people gamble with a fever that approaches religious zeal? Because, for some, gambling can be an act of pagan worship. And, the casinos can be analogous to pagan temples, complete with ritual, protocol, sacraments of alcohol, and even temple prostitution. With all the trappings and glitter of a pagan rite, gambling can involve an ultimate act of idolatry—placing oneself in the hands of Fortune and Destiny, the gods of chance.

Endnotes

1. American Psychiatric Association, *Diagnostic and Statistical Manual of Mental Disorders*, 3d ed. (Washington, D.C.: American Psychiatric Association, 1987), 324.

2. Robert Goodman, et. al., *Legalized Gambling as a Strategy for Economic Development*, United States Gambling Study, Center for Economic Development, University of Massachusetts, Amherst (March 1994): 93, 94.

3. *USA Today* (7 April 1991): 12-A.

4. *Casino Gambling: Panacea or Paradox?* (Mobile: Christian Life and Public Affairs Committee of the Mobile Baptist Association, 1992), 8.

5. Ibid., 4.

6. Arnold Wexler, *Arkansas Democrat* (26 December 1983).

7. "Regulation 1984," *Public Gaming* (February 1984): 18.

8. *Casino Gambling: Panacea or Paradox?*, 20.

9. Ibid., 20; See also Goodman, 92.

10. Ibid., 7.

11. Pam Schmid, "Problem Gambling Rising Among Teens, Some Experts Say," *Montgomery Advertiser* (12 January 1994): 2C.

12. Larry Braidfoot, *Gambling: A Deadly Game* (Nashville: Broadman, 1985), 156.

13. *Clarion-Ledger* (20 September 1992): 1-A.

14. Lorence, *Minnesota Lottery*, 31.

15. Ibid., 31.

16. Dr. Edmund Bergler, *Psychology of Gambling* (New York: Hill & Wang, 1957), 7.

17. Commission on the Review of the National Policy Toward Gambling, *Gambling in America*, 94th Cong., 2d sess., 1976, 436–8.

18. Lorence, *Minnesota Lottery,* 32.

19. *Gambling in America,* 417.

20. Goodman, *Legalized,* 60.

21. Aaron J. Rosanoff, *Manual of Psychiatry and Mental Hygiene* (New York: John Wiley & Sons, 1947), 138.

22. Maurice Parmalee, *Personality and Conduct* (New York: Moffatt, Yard & Co., 1918), 70.

23. Gereon Zimmermann, "Why?," *Look Magazine* (12 March 1963): 27.

Chapter Seven

Gambling and Crime

According to a 1982 Gallup poll, 71 percent of the American public believe legalized gambling will attract organized crime.[1]

Obviously, the fact that lots of people believe something doesn't make it true. But, widespread beliefs often have a basis in fact, and in this instance, the belief of the majority is clearly supported by the evidence.

We will examine the link between gambling and crime in four categories: (1) crimes committed by compulsive gamblers; (2) legal and illegal gambling; (3) corruption within legalized gambling systems; and, (4) gambling and organized crime.

Crimes Committed
by Compulsive Gamblers

We all know that drug addicts are often driven to theft and other crimes to obtain money to support their habits. The same is true of gambling addicts. As a 1977 study entitled *Gambling in Connecticut* observed, "When these men begin to lose big, as they must eventually, their financial situation becomes increasingly critical, leading them to steal, embezzle, and to arrange loans under fraudulent conditions to obtain the funds necessary to continue their gambling."[2]

The statistics bear this out. The gambling capital of the West, Nevada, consistently has the highest per capita rate of crime, divorce, and abortion. In 1981, the Las Vegas area was exceeded in reported crimes per capita only by Atlantic City and Miami. Prostitution (legal in some Nevada counties), alcohol, and drug abuse also rank high in Nevada and are associated with the gambling lifestyle and mindset.[3]

Atlantic City, New Jersey, is Las Vegas's counterpart in the East. Casinos were legalized in Atlantic City in 1978. The year before, 1977, 4,689 serious crimes were reported in Atlantic City. By 1985, these had more than tripled, to 14,914, even though the resident population of Atlantic City declined during that period by six thousand persons. Sixty-one percent of these crimes were committed in the casinos.[4]

Biloxi and Gulfport, Mississippi, seek to become the Las Vegas of the South. Casinos began in 1992 in Mississippi. The *Montgomery Advertiser* reports that the casinos have brought some tax revenue, but, at the same time, "crime rates have risen markedly. Property crimes, forgeries and theft cases all occur with much greater frequency. There have been eleven bank robberies so far this year, nearly twice as many as in the two previous years combined."[5]

Gerald T. Fulcher of the Delaware Council on Gambling Problems has estimated, based upon a federally funded study, that 86 percent of compulsive gamblers commit felony crimes to further their addiction.[6] Some compulsive gamblers resort to burglary, robbery, bad checks, etc., as means of raising money. Less noticed are those who engage in white collar crime: embezzlement, extortion, fraud, etc. The American Insurance Institute estimates that 40 percent of the nation's white collar crime is committed by compulsive gamblers, as well as 20 percent of spouse abuse.[7] The Connecticut Compulsive Gambling Treatment Center conducted a survey of judicial systems in 1983 and concluded 85 percent of the judicial systems reported that a proportion of white collar crime cases they deal with are related to gambling.[8]

Jordan Lorence gives a Minnesota example of white-collar crime:

> In 1981, the manager of a Golden Valley golf course pleaded guilty in Hennepin County District Court to embezzling about $65,000 from the golf course to support his gambling habit. Over the course of 3–

4 years, he wrote checks to nonexistent
employees and paid for goods never ordered by check. He cashed those checks,
and flew to Las Vegas with the money to
gamble. (Lorence, *Minnesota Lottery*, 29)

What if the golf course manager hadn't had
to fly to Las Vegas to gamble? What if (as is the
case now) casinos existed right home in Minnesota? The temptation would be much greater,
and such crimes would undoubtedly increase.
With the proliferation of casinos and other
forms of gambling in the 1980s and 1990s, the
shocking statistics cited above are, if anything,
low.

The free flow of alcohol is an integral part
of the gambling scene. Alcohol reduces inhibitions and, thus, encourages gamblers to risk
ever greater amounts. Recently, the New Jersey
legislature voted to prohibit free drinks at the
gaming tables, but spokesmen for the casinos
informed the legislature that they couldn't operate without free drinks. The lawmakers caved
in and reversed themselves, and drinks flow
freely once again in Atlantic City.[9] The free
consumption of alcohol reduces other inhibitions besides the urge to gamble and, thus, con-
tributes to crime.

Drugs are also part of the gambling scene.
An Arlington Park racetrack worker, who asked
not to be identified, recently told the *Horsemen's
Journal*, "I've been in jail before and it [the
racetrack] is a lot like that, everything controlled
and the guards are everywhere, but you can

still get anything you want. Give me 15 minutes and I can get you a pistol, a prostitute, or a pack of heroin."[10]

Likewise, prostitution goes hand in hand with gambling. It is estimated that there are ten thousand prostitutes actively plying their trade in Las Vegas alone,[11] and prostitution is rapidly increasing in Atlantic City and other cities that have legalized gambling. Like the casino operators, the prostitutes promise instant gratification of baser urges, and the presence of a pretty girl encourages an inebriated gambler to show off by risking more.

Combine these inhibition-reducing elements—gambling, alcohol, drugs, and prostitution—and you have a sure-fire formula for increased crime.

Legal and Illegal Gambling

The claim that legal gambling encourages illegal gambling sounds incredible to some. After all, why would someone choose to engage in illegal gambling when he can gamble legally instead?

But, in fact, wherever gambling is legalized, both legal and illegal gambling increase. As the Congressional study *Gambling in America* noted, "The mere presence of more opportunities to gamble increases the amount of gambling done. Moreover, the greater the total volume of gambling, the more favorable the environment is for the illegal operations."[12]

The study went on to say,

The Commission's research has shown that the availability of gambling creates new gamblers. A government that wishes merely to legitimize existing illegal wagering must recognize the clear danger that legalization may lead to unexpected and ungovernable increases in the size of the gambling clientele. (*Gambling in America*, 2)

Others confirm this conclusion. Don Thomas, Director of the St. Vincent-North Richmond Community Mental Health Center on Staten Island, says, "Atlantic City has swept many people into that lifestyle. The more available gambling, the more compulsive gamblers you will have."[13]

Dr. Valerie Lorenz of New Foundations, a Maryland compulsive gamblers' treatment center, says simply, "Social acceptance of gambling produces more gamblers."[14]

Since Connecticut legalized gambling, Austin McGuigan has prosecuted more than one thousand cases of illegal gambling. He says the evidence is "irrefutable" that legalized gambling causes increased illegal gambling.[15]

The Organized Crime Section of the Department of Justice concluded that "the rate of illegal gambling in those states which have some legalized form of gambling was three times as high as in those states" which do not have legalized gambling.[16]

And, Durand F. Jacobs, chief of Psychology Services at the Veterans Administration Hospital in Loma Linda, California, summarizes it well: "We have firm evidence to show that once a state promotes or endorses any kind of gambling, both legal and illegal forms of gambling accelerate."[17]

Their point is well taken. Morality, legality, and social acceptability are not the same, but they are definitely interrelated. A few people will gamble even if gambling is illegal. Some will refuse to gamble even if gambling is legal, either because their conscience tells them it is wrong or because their good sense tells them it is stupid.

But, in between, are a large number of people who equate morality, legality, and social acceptability. These people are likely to think, "How can gambling be wrong if the government makes it legal, or even runs and promotes it?"

And, when the gambling industry skillfully promotes a wholesome image for itself by pointing to all the respectable people who gamble, all the tax revenue raised, and all the worthwhile projects the industry supports, gambling loses its stigma and becomes almost a patriotic duty!

In this way, legalized gambling fosters a favorable climate for gambling as a whole, and legal and illegal gambling enterprises both benefit.

But, once again, why would anyone choose an illegal gambling operation when legal gambling is available instead?

There are a number of reasons which (at

least from a gambler's standpoint) make good sense:

1. The illegal operations offer better odds. They can afford to do so, partly because they don't pay taxes.

2. The illegal operators do not keep records and furnish them to the IRS and state tax authorities. The gambler can therefore avoid paying taxes on his winnings. (Under current federal law, gambling winnings are fully taxable, but gambling losses are deductible only to the extent that they do not exceed winnings.)

3. The illegal games commonly offer credit (and have their own ways of enforcing collection), while the legal games normally do not. For this reason, legal gamblers frequently switch to illegal gambling when their funds are exhausted.

4. The illegal games often have "numbers runners" who will come to the gambler's residence or place of business, take his money, buy a ticket, and return it to him.

5. The illegal operators often offer sports betting and other types of gambling that are not available through legal channels.

Lt. Robert Cantwell, a member of the Organized Crime Strike Force of the Colorado Attorney General's Office, summarized it well:

> The state must advertise a lottery to promote it. This creates a gambling appetite

in the people. Criminal gambling offers a better deal since the illegal operators offer credit, the convenience of runners, and no taxes. The illegal games have boosted their credibility by using the winning numbers of the legal game to select their winners. (Lorence, *Minnesota Lottery*, 27)

Corruption within Legalized Gambling Systems

Just legalize gambling, the industry spokesmen say, and we can clean it up and turn it into a respectable operation.

But, legalization does not remove the potential for corruption. Instances of employees stealing from the gambling operation persist. For example, in February 1981 a former lottery employee was convicted of fraud for stealing $8500 from the Ohio Lottery.[18]

Instances of rigging lotteries, or other gambling operations, also happen. In 1979, a former Connecticut Lottery employee who had rigged lottery drawings was convicted of obtaining money under false pretenses.[19]

In Pennsylvania in 1980, lottery winners were determined by an air blower which shoots up ping pong balls with numbers on them; the first three balls blown out constitute the winning number for the day. By injecting fluid into every ball except those numbered four and six, and then buying tickets with every combination of four and six, lottery personnel assured themselves of big winnings.[20]

In some states, among them Kansas and Missouri, losing tickets can be mailed in for special jackpot drawings. The problem is employees of stores which sell lottery tickets frequently collect the losing tickets that are discarded in the store and send them in. As Bob Mount of Overland Park, Kansas, complains, "They [the retailers] have an unlimited supply of free tickets. You don't have to be the FBI to figure out it's a tremendously unfair advantage."[21]

The racing industry is not immune from corruption either. As Larry Braidfoot demonstrates, among those practices common in the racing industry are the use of "ringers" (substituting fast horses for slow horses, or vice versa), illegal bookmaking, fraudulent use of the computer to alter the odds and skim money off the top, drugging animals to make them faster or slower, and the hiring of clerks and other personnel who have falsified their records and covered up past gambling convictions.[22] Detroit track owner Herbert Tyner, conceding that races probably had been fixed at his track, added, "Anybody would be naive if they believe that it does not happen, but it happens everywhere."[23]

The point is in a game that is based on the concept of getting-rich-quick, those on the inside will inevitably be tempted to cash in on the winnings themselves.

Gambling and Organized Crime

Director William Webster has declared succinctly that he knows of "no situation in which legalized gambling was in place where we did not eventually have organized crime."[24]

And, yet, every state that has legalized gambling has done so under the naive assumption that in their state the gambling industry will be "clean." The facts indicate that such hopes are unrealistic.

When New Jersey voters legalized casino gambling in 1976, Governor Brendan Byrne stood on the Boardwalk of Atlantic City and declared, "Organized crime is not welcome. I warn them, keep your filthy hands out of Atlantic City."[25]

But, eight years later a former aide of the governor admitted, "We were naive to think we could keep organized crime out. Now we recognize that the price of legalized gambling is that we become the focus of attention for undesirable elements."[26]

New Jersey Attorney General John Degnan put it bluntly: "But is organized crime present in Atlantic City? Yes. Is it there in greater force than it was before the casinos were passed? Yes. Are they trying to buy liquor licenses? Yes. Is there an increase in prostitution? Yes."[27]

> Anyone who goes into gambling should recognize, particularly in an urban center, that organized crime will be attracted to it like sharks to a bloated body. . . . Gambling provides a natural climate for that type of criminal element, and that's the price we're going to pay. (Zendzian, *Who Pays?*, 92)

And, despite New Jersey's determined efforts to keep organized crime out of Atlantic City, former New Jersey Attorney General William Hyland told a group of legislators: "I can tell you, gentlemen, that for every twenty-four hours you spend thinking about the problems of the state and how to combat organized crime, organized crime is spending a month figuring how to get around it . . . they are very resourceful and very clever."[28]

Why is organized crime attracted to gambling? Many crime figures may be attracted to the gambling lifestyle and all that goes with it. But, according to Dr. Craig Zendzian, a former New York police officer who spent much of his career investigating and studying organized crime, the basic answer is simple: "Gambling is, and always will be, a 'big money maker' for organized crime."[29] H. Clayton Waddell puts it this way, "The gold mine of the underworld is the gambling racket, and dimes and dollars from the pockets of ordinary, almost-honest citizens provide the gold."[30]

The City of Victoria, Australia, commissioned a Board of Inquiry to study the issues of casino gambling. The board examined the subject on an international basis and concluded that casino gambling is the lifeblood of organized crime because

> it provides an immense cash flow, it has considerable support services which can be taken over, it provides an entry into the top flight of the entertainment world, it

provides a secret but very efficient international banking system, it enables unlawful money to be laundered quickly and safely, it causes entry into the international hotel industry and it is causing money to flow from people who are unlikely to complain such as the compulsive gambler and naive persons. (Xavier Connor, *Report of Board of Inquiry into Casinos, City of Victoria, Australia* [Melbourne, Australia: F.D. Atkinson, Government Printer, 1983], 18)

Organized crime profits from gambling in many ways: by owning the casinos and thus taking in the profits, by "skimming" off the top (taking a "cut" before casino income is reported to the authorities), laundering money through the casinos, and owning or controlling the many industries that support and maintain the casinos, such as food services, hotels, manufacturers of gaming devices, banking, bonding, pawn shops, liquor, tobacco, etc.

In the 1940s, mobster Ben "Bugsy" Siegel spearheaded the building of Nevada's first luxury casino hotel, the Flamingo. The mob had sent Siegel to the West Coast to consolidate organized crime operations there and quickly gained notoriety as he developed relationships with famous movie celebrities. Siegel became convinced that nearby Nevada, having legalized most forms of gambling in 1931, could be a lucrative oasis for mob-run casinos. He persuaded eastern mob financiers to back the construction of the Flamingo, and it opened in

1946. Other mobsters began to suspect that Siegel was skimming profits, and on 20 June 1947, he was found shot to death in his home. Organized crime figures continued to be involved with the Flamingo and other Las Vegas casinos, and Zendzian traces Las Vegas casino connections with organized crime figures from New York, Chicago, Milwaukee, Cleveland, New Orleans, and Kansas City.[31]

In 1950, the Special Senate Committee to Investigate Organized Crime in Interstate Commerce, better known as the Kefauver Committee, reported, "It seems clear many of the men running gambling operations in Nevada are either members of existing out-of-state gambling syndicates or have histories of close association with the underworld characters who operate these syndicates."[32]

The 1976 congressional study, *Gambling in America*, concluded that in the previous ten years, the influence of organized crime on the Las Vegas casinos had declined somewhat due to strict state regulation. However, Eadington and others believe events since 1976 demonstrate that the influence of organized crime in Las Vegas is greater than the congressional study concluded.[33]

Unlike Las Vegas, where organized crime pioneered and controlled the gambling industry from the beginning, New Jersey officials tried to keep the mob out of the Atlantic City casinos. As we have noted above, and as New Jersey officials readily concede, their efforts were a failure. Nearly forty mob murders in Atlantic City between 1980 and 1986 are evidence of that.[34] The mob's tactic in Atlantic City was not so much ownership of the casinos, but rather through service industries. As U.S. Attorney W. Hunt Dumont observed, "Organized crime is insidious. It has found other ways to infiltrate the city—through the local unions, the Teamsters and construction unions and in subsidiary industries."[35] By controlling the industries that service gambling—transportation, hotels, food service, liquor, tobacco, drugs, prostitution—organized crime exerts a powerful influence upon the gambling industry.

Many Native American tribes have turned to gambling as a source of income, but even they are not immune to mob influence. As *U.S. News & World Report* noted in 1993:

> Now that 73 tribes in 19 states offer or will soon offer full-scale casino gambling, the big boys have taken notice. Atlantic City casino owner Donald Trump recently sued the U.S. government for allegedly giving an unfair advantage to tribes setting up casinos. And he's out to prove the fledgling industry is corrupt. "A lot of the reservations are being, at least to a certain extent, run by organized crime," says Trump. "There's no protection. It's become a joke." ("Gambling with the Mob? Wise Guys Have Set Their sights on the Booming Indian Casino Business," *U.S. News and World Report*, [23 August 1993]: 30)

Trump's charges have substance. In 1993, reputed Chicago organized crime figure John "No Nose" DiFronzo and his gambling expert, Donald "The Wizard of Odds" Angelini, were convicted of conspiracy and fraud for trying to take over gambling operations at the Rincon Reservation near San Diego.[36] And, *U.S. News* describes the U.S. Senate testimony of an organized crime figure:

> Seated in the largest Senate hearing room with a hood over his head to protect his identity, the witness identified only as "Marty" had some confessions to make. Not only had he helped the mob set up and run a high-stakes bingo hall on an Indian reservation, he testified, but he had padded expenses and robbed the tribe of over $600,000 a year.
>
> But even Marty's sensational tales of filling bingo balls with helium and awarding $60,000 cars to paid shills paled in comparison to his next news flash. Marty told members of the Senate Select Committee on Indian Affairs that twelve other Indian bingo halls also were controlled by the mob. "Organized crime is destroying the Indian reservation," he said in a slow, mechanical baritone, his voice deliberately altered through the use of a special machine. ("Gambling With the Mob?" 30)

When gambling gains a foothold, it begins to exert a powerful influence on state and local politics. Former Nevada Governor Grant Sawyer said in 1981 that "gaming is the most sensitive, important aspect of Nevada's government. . . . The gaming industry was, and still is, the major source of political campaign funds for all offices."[37]

The Kefauver Committee concluded that "the availability of huge sums of cash and the incentive to control political action resulted in gamblers and racketeers too often taking part in government. . . . Where gambling receives a cloak of respectability through legalization, there is no weapon which can be used to keep the gamblers out of politics."[38]

In Alabama, where gambling is a major political issue, the *Montgomery Advertiser* revealed that Democratic Governor Jim Folsom Jr. has received more than two hundred thousand dollars in campaign contributions from people or organizations with gambling ties, even though he promised in August 1993 that "my campaign will accept no contribution from any gaming interest or affiliate thereof."[39] As the *Advertiser* noted:

> That total includes at least $159,000 from political action committees controlled by a Montgomery lobbying firm that represents Mobile Greyhound Park; $30,000 from a shipbuilding company that's built floating casinos; and smaller contributions from other lobbyists who number gambling interests among their clients. (John D. Milazzo, "Folsom Funds Linked to Gambling," *Montgomery Advertiser* [24 February 1994]: 1–A)

When gambling is legalized, one may expect the gambling industry to use its profits to promote policies and conditions that are favorable to further gambling.

When we consider the link between gambling and crime—crimes committed by compulsive gamblers, illegal gambling, corruption of legalized gambling, and organized crime—it is appropriate to ask once again, Will legalized gambling really make your state and community a better place to live? Is this really the environment you want for yourself and your children?

Endnotes

1. Larry Braidfoot, *Gambling: A Deadly Game* (Nashville: Broadman, 1985), 85.

2. Jordan Lorence, *The Proposed Minnesota Lottery* (St. Paul: Berean League of Minnesota, 1984), 28.

3. William R. Eadington, "The Casino Gaming Industry: A Study of Political Economy," *The Annals* (July 1984): 32.

4. *The New Orleans Times-Picayune* (12 January 1986): 1, 18.

5. Editorial, "Gambling's Toll: Casinos Carry High Social Cost," *Montgomery Advertiser* (6 September 1993): 10-A.

6. Gerald T. Fulcher, "In Response: Legalized Gambling, Who Are Its Victims?" *State Legislatures* (October 1981): 20-1.

7. Ibid.

8. Lorence, *Minnesota Lottery*, 28–9.

9. *Casino Gambling: Panacea or Paradox?*, 8.

10. *The Horseman's Journal*, 1980, quoted by Robert Baker, Field Investigator, Department of Investigations, Humane Society of the United States, Testimony prepared for Texas State Legislature (8 March 1983): 5.

11. Craig A. Zendzian, *Who Pays? Casino Gambling, Hidden Interests, and Organized Crime* (New York: Harrow & Heston, 1993), 124.

12. Commission on the Review of the National Policy Toward Gambling, *Gambling in America*, 94th Cong., 2d sess., 1976, 161.

13. Lorence, *Minnesota Lottery*, 30.

14. Ibid., 31.

15. "Texans, Listen to This Expert," *The Family Educator* (Pro-Family Forum [Fall 1987]), 1.

16. Kerby Anderson, "Lotteries Bring Problems," *The Dallas [Texas] Morning News* (19 May 1984).

17. Sarah B. Ames, "Addiction Risk Linked to Lottery," *The Oregonian* (1 February 1987).

18. *Columbus Citizen-Journal* (8 July 1981): 1.

19. "Gambling Industry Reaps a Rich Harvest," *U.S. News & World Report* (25 August 1980): 38.

20. *St. Paul Dispatch* (9 December 1981): 6-A.

21. "Kansas Lottery Questioned," *Tulsa Tribune* (7 December 1987): B-2.

22. Braidfoot, *Gambling*, 89–92.

23. *Detroit News* (11 March 1984): 1-A, 10-A.

24. *The American Legion Magazine* (January 1985): 10-2.

25. Margaret Hornblower, "Atlantic City's Organized Crime Barrier Develops Major Issues," *Washington Post* (16 January 1984): 2.

26. Ibid.

27. Zendzian, *Who Pays?*, 124.

28. Ibid., 92.

29. Ibid., 1.

30. H. Clayton Waddell, "The Relationship Between Gambling and Crime," in *The Gambling Menace*, ed. Russ Coggins (Nashville: Broadman, 1966), 67.

31. See Zendzian, *Who Pays?* generally, esp. 19–22, 113–117.

32. *Gambling in America*, 80.

33. William R. Eadington, "The Casino Gaming Industry: A Study of Political Economy," *The Annals* (July 1984): 30.

34. *Parade Magazine* (11 May 1986): 14.

35. U.S. Attorney W. Hunt Dumont, quoted in "Atlantic City's Organized Crime Barrier Develops Major Fizzure" *The Washington Post* (16 January 1984): 2, 21.

36. "Gambling with the Mob? Wise Guys Have Set Their Sights on the Booming Indian Casino Business," *U.S. News and World Report* (23 August 1993): 30.

37. Zendzian, *Who Pays?*, 25.

38. Ibid., 24.

39. John D. Milazzo, "Folsom Funds Linked to Gambling," *Montgomery Advertiser* (24 February 1994): 1-A.

Chapter Eight

Gambling and Cruelty to Animals

From 1981 to 1990, our family lived in Oklahoma. (After accepting a professorship at the Thomas Goode Jones School of Law in Montgomery, I described my Oklahoma years as the "halfway house" between my old life in the Upper Midwest and my new life in Alabama.)

During the 1980s Oklahoma was the subject of a campaign to legalize pari-mutuel betting on horse racing. The campaign was well-financed and professionally orchestrated. Large billboards on the highways proclaimed exuberantly, "Let's Race!" Country western singer Roy Clark of "Hee Haw" fame, who owns a large ranch in Oklahoma, appeared on television commercials saying wistfully, "I sure love my horses. But I can't race'em. Not in Oklahoma."[1]

The implication was that anyone who did not support pari-mutuel betting was not fond of horses. And, in horse country like Oklahoma, that's just plain unpatriotic!

Let me set the record straight. I own both horses and dogs, and I am a lover of both. In fact, that's part of the reason I oppose pari-mutuel betting.

And, the fact is, Roy Clark was free to race his horses in Oklahoma any time he wanted to. All he couldn't do was bet on them. The "Let's Race!" billboards should have read, "Let's Gamble!"

The horse racing industry presents itself as a great fraternity of horse lovers. But, as Tom Brokaw said on "NBC Nightly News" in May 1984, "There is another side of horse racing, however, so sinister and so corrupting that it is now the target of a major federal investigation. It is horse doping, and it has become a big business."[2]

Horse doping takes place to fix races by stimulating some horses to run faster and slowing others down. Other drugs like Lasix are used to cause fluid and weight loss and to prevent fluid and blood pressure on the lungs in horses known as "bleeders." As Andrew Beyer, racing columnist for the *Washington Post*, explains:

When racing commissions in Maryland and other states were debating the legalization of Lasix, veterinarians appeared as expert witnesses. They were so determined to win approval of the drug that their testimony was not completely candid.

They assured commissions that Lasix wouldn't affect a horse's form, when every bettor knew otherwise. They didn't insist that a Lasix program had to be accompanied by adequate safeguards—a detention barn, a top testing laboratory—or it could be used to hide the presence of illegal drugs in a horse's system.

One well-informed vet said there is a typical route for narcotics to reach the track. They are usually developed by European chemical companies; they are used first at quarter-horse tracks where, in the common view, anything goes. If they are effective, they wind up in thoroughbred racing. (Andrew Beyer, "Vets and Their Drugs: Racing the Nightmare," *Washington Post* (12 December 1984): B–2)

One problem with Lasix is that it has a masking effect; it makes it difficult to detect illegal drugs in a horse's system.[3] The same is true of Butazolodin, an anti-inflammatant and painkiller administered to horses.[4]

Painkillers present a special problem because they make it possible to race horses that have sprains, fractures, or other injuries and are in no condition to run. As Texans Who Care observes, "Horses, too, are often maimed—even killed—in on-track 'breakdowns.' New super-pain-killers mean that many horses, forced to run with injuries, simply collapse during the race with broken or shattered legs. Over 2000 of such hopelessly crippled horses must be killed every year."[5]

Similar cruelty exists in dog racing. Did you ever wonder why dogs, who are far more oriented toward scent than toward vision, will follow an electric rabbit around a track? Most dogs wouldn't pay any attention to an artificial rabbit; they have to be trained to do so as a conditioned response.

As Texans Who Care observe:

> Dog racing is a true bloodsport. 90% of greyhound trainers use live lures—usually rabbits, sometimes even kittens—teaching the normally peaceful dogs to catch the living bait and rip it to shreds. 100,000 small animals die this traumatic death each year. The dogs themselves fare no better. Over 30,000 greyhounds are slaughtered each year because they've stopped making a profit for their owners or because they don't show enough potential to do so. (*Behind the Images: Inside Dog and Horse Racing* [flyer published by Texans Who Care]).

As Robert O. Baker, field investigator for the Humane Society of the United States, reports:

> It is obvious that dog racing as it exists today is nothing other than a "blood sport"

since greyhounds are allowed to attack and viciously kill other animals. The major difference between greyhound racing and dog and cockfighting is that this "blooding" is done behind the scenes in dog racing. (*Behind the Images* [flyer published by Texans Who Care]).

Let us dispel, once and for all, the myth that pari-mutuel betting is the sport of those who love dogs and horses. Rather, it is the business of those who cruelly exploit dogs and horses for profit.

Christians, while God gave man dominion over the beasts of the earth (Gen. 1:26, 28), He certainly does not want us to exploit and misuse His creatures in this way.

And, animal rights advocates, are you listening?

Endnotes

1. Roy Clark, commercials on Oklahoma television, 1980s. The words reflect the essence of Mr. Clark's message but are not intended to be a verbatim quotation.

2. *Behind the Images: Inside Dog and Horse Racing* (flyer published by Texans Who Care [Dallas, Texas]).

3. Robert O. Baker, testimony before Subcommittee on Criminal Justice, House Committee on the Judiciary, 97th Congress (Government Printing Office, 1983), Serial No. 137.

4. Ibid.; See also Sylvia Phillips, "Running for Their Lives: The Ugly Side of Greyhound Racing," *The Animal's Agenda* (May 1986): 10ff; Humane Society President John Hoyt, "Why We Oppose Greyhound Racing," *Humane Society News* (Winter 1985) (reprint).

5. *Behind the Images.*

Chapter Nine

A Winnable War:
We *Can* Defeat Gambling!

The gambling industry likes to surround itself with an aura of invincibility. As an ad for a state-run lottery in Massachusetts says, "Don't try to fight it. It's bigger than you are."[1] Eugene Martin Christiansen, a leading gambling industry consultant though not necessarily a gambling advocate, says:

> There is a general move toward legal casino-type games. It is part of a fundamental change that is irreversible at this point because the country is changing with fewer people going to church, more older people with time and money on their hands, and especially with state lottery advertising cam-

paigns that make it seem that buying lottery tickets is almost a patriotic duty. (Eugene Martin Christiansen, *Sun Herald* [18 October 1992]: A-1)

As the gambling epidemic seems to be sweeping the country, some are likely to think that, since it is inevitable that gambling will be legalized, why fight it? Our community, or our state, may as well get in line and cash in on our share of the profits.

I do not believe tides of history are irreversible. People shape historical trends, and with God's help, people can change them.

As we saw in chapter 2, gambling was common in the ancient pagan world, but the Church successfully campaigned against it. Gambling was common in early America, but church people and other civic-minded citizens put an end to it.

Right now the tide is surging toward a nation of gamblers. But, we can reverse that tide! Let me suggest some practical means of winning the war against gambling.

Be Informed!

Read this book thoroughly, and be prepared to present the information contained herein intelligently.

The National Coalition Against Legalized Gambling, 2376 Lakeside Drive, Birmingham, Alabama, 35244, (205) 985-9062, also publishes good information on the subject. They would welcome your inquiry.

Gamblers Anonymous helps compulsive gamblers overcome their addiction, and they can provide helpful information. They can be reached at P.O. Box 17173, Los Angeles, California, 90017, (213) 386-8789, and they can put you in touch with the nearest local chapter. The Christian Life Commission of the Southern Baptist Convention, 901 Commerce #550, Nashville, Tennessee, 37203, (615) 244-2495, has taken the lead in fighting the gambling industry and has produced much valuable literature. Likewise, the various state and local Christian Life Commissions of the Southern Baptist Convention have produced good material. Gambling proponents may attack Baptist sources as biased, but they generally use good and thorough documentation. When I am challenged for using a Baptist publication, I usually respond by asking my opponent to show any inaccuracies in the Baptist publication. This usually silences these critics.

In addition, it is important to keep up with current developments in your state or community. You may wish to clip these and keep a file or looseleaf binder notebook.

Speak Out!

Just being informed is not enough. To make a difference on this issue, you must get involved and speak out in your community.

Letters to the editor, letters to your legislators, and calls to local talk shows are a good—and free—means of spreading the message. It is

best to keep your messages brief and courteous
and be sure you have your information straight
and can back up your statements with solid
sources. Let me suggest a few tips for commu-
nicating your message effectively:

The content and style of your message must
vary with your audience—not that the truth
changes, but you use the arguments which are
most likely to score points with your audience
and the style that is most likely to establish
rapport with them.

Churches and Sunday school classes are excellent places to share this information, for gambling is clearly a moral issue with Scriptural
implications. Most church audiences—even
Catholic and mainline Protestant churches—are
likely to be sympathetic to your message, but
many are uninformed on the issue and fail to
see the Scriptural and moral implications of
gambling.

In speaking to these audiences you should
stress the Scriptural and moral arguments set
forth in chapter 3, but it is also important to go
beyond these and address the social, economic,
and criminal aspects of gambling. Christian
audiences should not be placed in the dilemma
of choosing between that which is morally right
and that which is economically advantageous.
When that choice arises, we should of course
choose that which is morally right. But, that is
a false dilemma here; gambling is neither morally right nor economically advantageous.

Speaking to non-church audiences requires

a different approach. If you handle it right, these are excellent opportunities to get your message across. If you don't, it can backfire.

Groups like Rotary, Kiwanis, Sertoma, etc., are often looking for programs for their meetings. Program chairmen for these groups often look for controversial issues because these arouse interest and increase attendance. The membership of these groups is usually made up of civic-minded citizens and community leaders, so this is an excellent opportunity to influence public opinion. But, you have to handle it right.

Gambling advocates like to paint their opponents as uninformed religious zealots who quote the Bible and do nothing else. When a well-informed opponent of gambling comes armed with solid facts and statistics about the social, economic, and criminal aspects of gambling, this throws them off guard and makes an excellent presentation.

This doesn't necessarily mean you should avoid the moral issues. Rather than stressing the biblical points, however, it is often best to stress the moral objections that make sense to Christians and non-Christians alike. The fact that gambling preys upon the poor, involves getting rich at someone else's expense while giving nothing in return, and causes cruelty to animals has a moral impact upon practically everyone with good moral values.

As noted, the persons who make up these organizations are usually decent, civic-minded citizens who are concerned about the well-being of their families and communities. The quality-of-life argument usually strikes home with them. Ask them if they really want their city to become another Las Vegas or Atlantic City.

Radio talk shows are also a good way of getting the message across. Often talk show hosts are looking for good guests. If a spokesman for the gambling industry appears on a talk show, you might call the host afterward and ask if he would consider giving you equal time. You might be surprised at how often the response will be positive. On the show, just relax and answer the questions in a normal conversational tone.

Likewise, newspaper editors—even those of the opposite persuasion—are often willing to print guest editorials if they are responsible, succinct, and well-written.

Another point to remember about communication: Some people are impressed with statistics; others are impressed with real-life examples—especially if they involve people within your personal knowledge. The example of the nineteen-year-old boy who lost six thousand dollars on a lottery drawing and attempted suicide rather than facing his parents[2] may speak more profoundly to some listeners than a dozen statistics because they can imagine their own child or grandchild doing the same thing.

It is important to challenge the claims of gambling advocates. Often, they will present rosy projections of the tourists attracted, jobs created, and revenue generated by their casinos and racetracks. Remember, they want to get their foot in the door and will promise almost anything and agree to almost anything—at first. Afterward, their demands change. For example, gambling advocates desperately wanted dog racing in Alabama, and they promised that the racetrack would produce jobs and revenue. Now, the gambling industry tells us the racetracks will go broke unless they can offer casinos, lotteries, and horse racing as well.[3]

When Iowa legalized riverboat gambling in 1989, the state limited the size of bets to five dollars and anyone's losses to two hundred dollars per night. Now, riverboat owners are telling the Iowa legislature that they can't make a profit under those limitations, and, unless the limitations are relaxed, they will float their riverboats downstream to some place like Mississippi.[4] Supposedly, this is necessary to compete with riverboats from Illinois, just like expanded gambling in Alabama is necessary to compete with Mississippi. But, if Iowa and Alabama meet these demands, what will Illinois and Mississippi do next? The never-ending competition and improved technology produces ever-escalating spirals of higher stakes, new forms of gambling, and more exotic and unwholesome enticements to go with it.

This book contains valuable ammunition that can persuade people that gambling is not a good idea. Copies of this book may be ordered at discount prices from the publisher, Huntington House; (800) 749-4009.

Also, the author of this book has produced a color video lecture, about forty-five minutes in length, which is suitable for showing in churches or civic groups. The video features the biblical and moral case against gambling, the regressive nature of gambling, the economic problems of gambling, the dangers of gambling addiction, the criminal aspects of gambling, and the cruelty to animals which occurs in racing. This video is available for a cost of twenty dollars, postage included, and may be obtained by writing to the author, John Eidsmoe, c/o Jones School of Law, 5345 Atlanta Highway, Montgomery, AL, 36193.

Don't Gamble Yourself!

By gambling yourself, you give grounds for impeaching your own credibility.

What about minor bets among individuals? Is it really wrong to bet twenty-five cents per hole on a golf game or ten cents per hand on a game of gin rummy or an evening of bingo for minor stakes for a church or charity? If you can afford to lose a buck or two, and it makes the game more exciting, what's wrong with that? Or, what about buying a raffle ticket to support a charitable institution?

I will leave these questions to your own individual judgment. You might consider, however, that such seemingly innocent activity could lead to an unhealthy interest in gambling and could cause you or others to conclude that other forms of gambling are otherwise acceptable.

And, if you really need a money bet to make the game of golf or gin rummy exciting, you might consider switching to a different hobby. What do you do when someone asks you to buy a raffle ticket for a charity? You don't want to compromise your convictions, but you also don't want to seem cheap or judgmental. Here's one way of handling the situation. Recently, one of my law students asked me to buy a one dollar raffle ticket for a worthwhile organization; the prize was a color television set. I told him I was morally opposed to raffles because they are a form of gambling, and I briefly explained why. I then gave him a dollar as a contribution to his organization, without buying the ticket. I made my point, avoided appearing cheap or judgmental, contributed to a worthwhile cause, and perhaps showed my student and his group that there are other means of raising money. (But, I still can't help wondering if I would have won that television set!)

Seek Organizational Support!

To be effective politically, working strictly on your own usually is not enough. To really make a difference, it is usually necessary to work in concert with others.

Working with the political party of your choice is one way of making an impact. In most states, party precinct, county, and state organizations adopt resolutions and platforms on the issues of the day. These official positions of the party draw the attention of the media and are considered by lawmakers as they ponder legislation.

Resolutions by church bodies also help to solidify support for a position. The church we attend, Trinity Presbyterian Church (PCA) of Montgomery, Alabama, adopted the following resolution at the 27 September 1993 meeting of the Session (the church's governing body):

RESOLUTION

BE IT RESOLVED by the Session of Trinity Presbyterian Church as follows:

WHEREAS, the issues of potential casino gambling, a state-run lottery and other forms of legalized gambling are detrimental to the people of the state of Alabama and are in contravention of the teaching of God's word; and

WHEREAS, it is felt that expansion of legalized gambling in the state of Alabama will be especially damaging and corrupting to the young people of the state of Alabama and will also be destructive of additional homes and communities; and

WHEREAS, the Session of Trinity Presbyterian Church would like to go on record as being opposed to legalized gambling in the state of Alabama; NOW, THEREFORE, BE IT RESOLVED by the Session of Trinity Presbyterian Church that this Session hereby goes on record as being opposed to all forms of commercial gambling, in that they are detrimental to the young people and families of the state of Alabama and this Session further goes on record as being adamantly opposed to any further expansion of legalized gambling in the State of Alabama. ("Session Takes Stand Against Gambling," Bulletin, Trinity Presbyterian Church, Montgomery, Alabama, 17 October 1993)

Resolutions might have broader, but less focused, effect if adopted by district or national denominational conventions.

In 1984, the Southern Baptist Convention adopted the following resolution:

RESOLUTION ON GAMBLING

WHEREAS, Gambling is an immoral effort that creates deliberate risks not inherent in or necessary to the functioning of society; and

WHEREAS, Aggressive actions by the gambling interests in recent months make abundantly clear their intention of seeking to expand legalized gambling throughout the nation and especially in the states of the South and the Southwest; and

WHEREAS, Out-of-state corporations and businesses are investing millions of dollars in a bold effort to change state laws to allow casinos, lotteries, and pari-mutuel gambling; and

WHEREAS, Legislators of many states have shown shameful willingness to give shoddy and inadequate consideration to gambling legislation, to pass legislation out of committees without public hearings, and to schedule votes of gambling legislation in a manner carefully contrived to be beneficial to passage of the gambling legislation.

Be it therefore Resolved, That we, as messengers of the Southern Baptist Convention assembled in Kansas City, June 12–14, 1984, encourage Southern Baptists to work diligently with other Christians and other responsible citizens who oppose the spread of legalized gambling; and

Be it further Resolved, That we encourage the churches and the state conventions cooperating with the Southern Baptist Convention to engage in vigorous programs of education for adults, teenagers, and children about the moral tragedies wrought by legalized gambling; and

Be it further Resolved, That we express our prayerful support and strong encouragement for those who are providing courageous leadership in vigorously opposing the legalization of gambling both in the states where votes are scheduled and at the national level where pressure is building in support of legalized gambling.

Be it finally Resolved, That we express our grave concern that gambling interests have unscrupulously twisted the decision of the 1983 Southern Convention Baptist Convention in 1989 to imply that Southern Baptists are compromising their opposition to gambling, and that we declare to gambling interests and to the world that our purpose for meeting in Las Vegas is an expression of our mission to give support to Baptist work and to share Christ with the people of that area; and that we affirm our opposition to gambling regardless of any choice of site for a Convention meeting. (Larry Braidfoot, *Gambling: A Deadly Game* [Nashville: Broadman, 1985], 219-20)

These resolutions could serve as good models for similar resolutions by your church or denomination.

Involvement by other organizations—especially groups not normally regarded as politically activist or aligned with conservative Christian positions—can be especially helpful in solidifying community support. For example, on 8 September 1993, the Alabama Sheriffs' Association adopted a resolution opposing casino gambling and any liberalization of the state's gambling laws. The resolution stated that Alabama sheriffs, charged with protecting citizens against crime, "recognize the inherent evil and risk to the public which would be posed by organized gambling."[5]

Resolutions by other groups, such as education groups concerned about the effect of gambling upon children, could solidify other elements of the community.

Form Coalitions!

All too often, political activists tend to associate only with those who share their views on every issue. This is especially true of conservative Christians.

Understandable though this may be, it is self-defeating. By associating only with those who share your views on every issue, you cut yourself off from many potential allies, some of whom might be very effective in the fight against legalized gambling.

For example, in Oklahoma in the 1980s, church groups and the horse racing industry squared off against each other on the issue of pari-mutuel betting. After a heated battle, the horse racing industry won.

Shortly thereafter, a campaign began to establish a state-run lottery in Oklahoma. Church groups fighting the lottery found an unexpected ally—the horse racing industry! Concerned that competition from the lottery might cut into their profits and drive the racetracks out of business, the horse racing industry joined the campaign against lotteries. And, because their economic survival was at stake, they were willing to put their money and public relations expertise into the campaign. So far, the lottery has been stopped cold in Oklahoma!

Other groups not normally associated with conservative causes might join the fight against legalized gambling:

- Animal rights groups concerned about

cruelty to animals in racing, as detailed in chapter 8.

• Feminist groups concerned about the exploitation of women as prostitutes, strippers, and bar-girls in the casinos and the increase of female compulsive gamblers.

• Consumer groups concerned about fraud in casinos.

• Anti-crime interests concerned about the links between gambling and crime.

• Anti-liquor and anti-drug groups, since liquor and drugs commonly accompany legalized gambling.

• Civil rights groups concerned about exploitation of minority groups through legalized gambling.

• Those who work for the relief of poor people since gambling is a regressive form of taxation that preys upon the poor.

• Mental health groups concerned about the spread of compulsive gambling and other accompanying addictions.

• Environmentalist groups concerned about the effect of casinos and racetracks upon the environment.

• Business groups concerned about the effect of gambling upon legitimate businesses.

• Educators and others who work with youth, recognizing the rise of teenage compulsive gamblers.

• Community betterment groups concerned about the overall effect of gambling upon the quality of life in the community.

By building coalitions on specific issues, a working majority can be developed to defeat legalized gambling. And, possibly a basis for communication and bridge-building on other issues may be developed as well.

Oppose Referenda!

When gambling advocates fail to get their proposals through the legislature, they commonly call for a referendum, or a direct vote of the people. Most states allow popular referenda, though the means of obtaining one vary from state to state.

Calls for popular referenda are difficult to resist. After all, who could possibly be opposed to a vote of the people? Isn't that the democratic way? What are you afraid of—you might lose?

Don't fall for this ploy. There are good reasons to oppose a popular referendum on gambling.

For one thing, a referendum campaign is extremely expensive. To take a campaign directly to the people, one must spend money extensively on radio and television advertising, direct mailings, billboards, yard signs, bumper stickers, and the like. In various referenda throughout the nation, the gambling industry has commonly outspent their opponents many times over. They are willing to do so because they have a direct financial interest in the outcome. It is to the shame of Christians and others who hold traditional values that they are not willing to match the gambling interests dollar-for-dollar, but it is a fact of life.

Second, the Founders of our nation established a constitutional republic, not a pure democracy in the sense of unfettered absolute majority rule. One basic principle of a constitutional republic is that the people govern, not directly by popular vote, but rather through elected representatives.

Occasionally, when legislators are not responsive to the will of the people, a referendum is appropriate as a popular check on abuse of government power. Normally, though, drafting and passing laws and policies is the job of legislators. That's what we elect them for.

Support a Crackdown on Gambling!

If gambling is illegal in your state but various forms are being carried on anyway, demand enforcement of the laws. You may need to use trial and error until you find out which prosecutors and which law enforcement officials are sympathetic to your position and are willing to enforce the law.

If various forms of gambling are legalized in your state, you can work for the enactment and enforcement of measures to limit the effects of gambling:

• Taxes on the gambling industry should be as high as possible. This increases the price of gambling and discourages potential gamblers. Likewise, the winnings of gamblers should continue to be taxable; efforts of the gambling industry to make gambling winnings tax-exempt (ostensibly so legalized gambling can compete with illegal gambling) should be resisted. After all, we don't exempt liquor stores from taxation so they can compete with moonshiners!

• The gambling industry should be strictly regulated, and they themselves should be required to shoulder the cost of that regulation. Those seeking licenses to run gambling establishments should undergo careful background checks, at their expense.

• Strict limits should be applied to the amount one may wager and the amount one may lose in an evening.

• Complimentary cocktails should be illegal at gambling establishments, and strict limits should be placed on the number of drinks that can be served. If the gambling establishments insist they cannot operate profitably without the free flow of liquor, they are saying in effect that people won't gamble sufficiently unless alcohol has affected the customers' judgment.

• Prostitution and stripshows should be strictly prohibited at gambling establishments, and these prohibitions should be strictly enforced. These vices are part of the general atmosphere that reduces inhibitions and brings out the gambling urge.

• Laws should be adopted and enforced which impose strict penalties for admitting minors into gambling establishments. One way of ensuring that gambling establishments honor these laws is to require casinos to reimburse minors for any gambling losses incurred in their establishments.

• Strict penalties should be imposed for cruelty to animals in dog and horse racing.

• City and state governments should not finance casinos and racetracks, either by government grants or loans or by municipal bonds.

Pray!

While people are granted some degree of freedom to influence human affairs, I believe God is sovereign and that He uses events through his sovereign superintending power to work out His will for the human race. Normally, He chooses to work through people. Pray that God's will be done, and make yourself an instrument He can use to accomplish His will.

> Be not ye afraid of them: remember the Lord, which is great and terrible, and fight for your brethren, your sons, and your daughters, your wives, and your houses. (Neh. 4:14)

Endnotes

1. Robert Goodman, et. al., *Legalized Gambling as a Strategy for Economic Development*, United States Gambling Study, Center for Economic Development, University of Massachusetts, Amherst (March 1994): 135.

2. Larry Braidfoot, *Gambling: A Deadly Game* (Nashville: Broadman, 1985), 155.

3. Milton E. McGregor, "Alabama Will Get 24,000 New Jobs," *The Economic Gazette*, vol. I, no. 1, (August 1993): 5.

4. Rita Koselka and Christopher Palmeri, "Snake Eyes," *Forbes* (1 March 1993): 70–1.

5. John D. Milazzo, "Sheriffs Oppose Expanded Gambling," *Montgomery Advertiser* (9 September 1993): 1-A, 6-A.

Appendix

Preachers and Politics:
What Does the IRS Allow?

(Churches and other nonprofit organizations are likely to take the lead in the battle against legalized gambling. However, many are hesitant to get involved because of concern over their tax-exempt status. To help pastors, churches, and other nonprofit organizations understand what types of political activities they may and may not engage in without jeopardizing their tax-exempt status, John Eidsmoe prepared the following article for American Vision in 1988. We appreciate American Vision's kind permission to reproduce a revised version of that article.)

Preaching on politics is as American as apple pie. The Father of the American Revolution,

Samuel Adams, used to call the New England clergy his "black regiment" because he could count on them to proclaim the message of liberty and independence from the pulpits across the land. Early American clergymen commonly preached "election sermons" near election day to remind their parishioners of their civic responsibilities and to present a biblical view of political affairs. The French observer, Alexis de Tocqueville, wrote that while religion in America takes no direct part in government it "must be regarded as the first of their political institutions."

This is not surprising. God's Word has a lot to say about abortion, crime and punishment, economics, national defense, foreign policy, and almost every other issue one can imagine. The preacher who fails to present the biblical viewpoint on these matters is not preaching the whole counsel of God. For civil government is, as Paul tells us in Romans 13, ordained by God. In all his voluminous works, Martin Luther wrote more about civil government than any other subject except justification by faith. For this reason, if the United States Government were to prohibit pastors from preaching on political issues or churches from engaging in political activity, it would not only violate the First Amendment guarantee of free speech; it would also, in my opinion, violate the First Amendment guarantee of free exercise of religion. While the religious beliefs of some pastors do not compel them to speak out on political issues, the religious beliefs of others do.

Our government has not prohibited churches from engaging in political activity. But through the IRS, it has done something similar: It has required churches to curtail sharply their political activity or lose their 501(c)(3) tax-exempt status. While this is not an outright prohibition on political activity, the effect is similar. The U.S. Supreme Court noted in *McCulloch v. Maryland*, 17 U.S. (4 Wheat.) 316 (1819), "The Power to tax involves the power to destroy." And as the Supreme Court also noted in *United States v. Butler*, 297 U.S. 1 (1936), "[T]he power to confer or withhold unlimited benefits is the power to coerce or destroy."

My position, then, is that the current restrictions on political activity by religious organizations are an unconstitutional infringement on religious freedom. I hope they will be changed. But the main purpose of this article is not to argue what the law should be, but to explain what the law *is*—so that pastors and church workers can be informed and act accordingly to preserve their tax-exempt status, if they are so inclined.

Let us begin by noting that merely incorporating a nonprofit corporation under the laws of your state does not automatically make you a tax-exempt organization in the eyes of the IRS.

To obtain tax-exempt status, most organizations must file for such status under Section 501(c)(3) of the Internal Revenue code. Many are unaware, however, that churches need not file under Sec. 501(c)(3); a church has such status automatically simply by being a church unless the IRS revokes such tax-exempt status for various code violations.

Generally speaking though, churches are tax-exempt organizations under 501(c)(3) of the Internal Revenue Code. This means they do not have to pay taxes on their income, and persons who donate to such churches can deduct their contributions from their taxable income. But in order to obtain and retain their tax-exempt status, the Internal Revenue Code requires that churches and other organizations must be "organized and operated exclusively for religious, charitable, scientific, testing for public safety, or educational purposes . . ." In keeping with this requirement, the Code limits political activity in two ways: (1) "No substantial part of the activities of which is carrying on propaganda, or otherwise attempting, to influence legislation;" and, (2) the organization must "not participate in or intervene in (including the publishing or distributing of statements), any political campaign on behalf of any candidate for public office."

You'll notice two categories of political activity: (1) Attempting to influence legislation. This is allowed to some degree; the Code simply says no "substantial part" of the organization's activities may be directed to influencing legislation. (But what is "substantial"?—Good question. We'll discuss that later.) And, (2) Participating in campaigns for public office.

There is no substantiality rest here; this is prohibited entirely.

Let's discuss each of these categories separately:

Influencing Legislation

As we have seen no substantial part of the church's activities may be directed toward influencing legislation. But several questions arise: (a) What is legislation? (b) What constitutes influencing legislation? (c) What is substantial?

(a) Legislation consists of laws passed by a legislative body, whether it is Congress, your state legislature, a local county commission or city council. It does not include action by an administrative body such as a school board or zoning commission. Nor does it normally include action by an executive; for example, a letter to the president urging him to follow a certain course of action such as bombing Iraq is not influencing legislation. If, however, the president is preparing legislation to present to Congress, communications with his staff concerning that proposed legislation might constitute influencing legislation.

Urging the courts to take action normally does not constitute influencing legislation. Also, you are not influencing legislation if you simply urge that existing laws be enforced; for example, a letter to the mayor or police chief urging that existing laws be used to crack down on pornography, is not influencing legislation. See IRS Reg. 1.501(c)(3)-1(c)(3)(ii); IRS Reg. 53.4945-

(2)(a)(2); IRS Reg. 53.4945-2(a)(2); Rev. Rul. 73-440, 1973-2 C.B. 177; Rev. Rul. 67-293, 1967-2 C.B. 185.

(b) What is influencing legislation? The IRS considers "direct lobbying" to be influencing legislation. Direct lobbying consists of communications with members of employees of legislative bodies or government officials who may participate in the formulation of legislation, which pertains to legislation being considered by a legislative body and reflects a view with respect to the desirability of the legislation. See IRS Reg. 1.501(c)(3)1(c)(3)(ii).

The IRS also prohibits 501(c)(3) organizations from engaging substantially in another form of influencing legislation called "grassroots lobbying," which consists of urging the public to support or oppose legislation. See proposed IRS Reg 56.4911-2(c).

Even if you do not expressly urge the public to contact their legislators, your expression of opinion concerning the desirability or undesirability of legislation might be considered lobbying.

Activity that primarily seeks to inform people about an issue is not considered as influencing legislation, even if it involves taking a position on the issue. As the Court of Claims said in *Haswell v. United States*, 500 F2d 1133 (1974),

> Advocacy of a particular position or viewpoint qualifies as nonpartisan analysis, study, or research as long as there is a sufficiently full and fair exposition of the

pertinent facts to enable the public or an individual to form an independent opinion or conclusion.

If you state your opinions in a reasonably objective manner, presenting both sides of the issue, your activity is more likely to be viewed as educational rather than influencing legislation. It is also more likely to be viewed as religious activity if it is geared toward presenting what the Bible has to say about a political issue—which is what we should be stressing anyway. However, we still have to be careful. As the Tenth Circuit Court of Appeals said in *Christian Echoes National Ministry, Inc., v. United States*, 470 F2d 849 (1972), "The fact that specific legislation was not mentioned does not mean that these attempts to influence public opinion were not attempts to influence legislation."

The IRS recognizes a "technical advice" exception. If your organization supplies technical expertise in response to a request by a governmental body, this will not constitute influencing legislation. The request, however, must come from a governmental body, and not simply from an individual legislator. For example, if Senator Johnson were to ask the Director of the Rutherford Institute to testify before the Senate Education Committee as to the constitutionality of a creation-science bill, that would be influencing legislation. But if Senator Johnson could get the Senate Education Committee itself to formally make the request, that would not constitute influencing legislation. See IRS

Code 4911 and 4945(e)(2); IRS Reg. 53.4945-2(d)(2). This regulation provides that the request must be made in the name of the legislative body and not the individual legislator, that your response must be available to every member of the requesting legislative body, and your opinions and recommendations may be offered only if they are specifically requested by the legislative body.

The IRS also recognizes a "self defense" exception: If legislative action is proposed which might affect the existence of your organization, its powers and duties, its tax-exempt status, or deductibility of contributions to the organization. For example, suppose you are director of The Yellowstone Park Mission Society, an organization that holds religious services and conducts witnessing in Yellowstone National Park. Suppose further, a bill is proposed in Congress which would prohibit the holding of religious services or giving out religious literature in national parks. Since that bill directly affects the existence and activities of your organization, your efforts to defeat the bill will probably be considered an exception to the prohibition against influencing legislation. The same might be true of bills to provide for taxation of church property, etc. See IRC 4911(d)(2)(D); IRC 4945(e); IRS Reg. 53.4945(2)(d)(3)(i)&(ii).

Section 4911(d)(2)(D) exempts from the lobbying prohibition certain communications between an organization and its members. According to Proposed IRS Reg. 56.4911-5(b), such communications must be (1) directed only to the membership; (2) related to legislation of direct interest to the organization and its members; and (3) not directly encourage the members to engage in direct or grassroots lobbying. Members are defined as those who pay dues or make more than nominal contributions ("nominal" is not defined) or those who are of a limited number or honorary or life members who have been chosen for valid reasons such as length or service or involvement in organizational activities.

According to IRS Code Section 4945, examinations and discussions of broad social, economic, and similar issues do not constitute influencing legislation so long as they do not address specific legislative proposals, even if these are the types of issues legislatures are likely to address. IRS Reg. 53.4945-2(d)(4) attempts to clarify this, but this exception is still very vague.

But, even if your activity does constitute "express advocacy" of legislation, it will not affect your tax-exempt status if it does not constitute a "substantial portion" of your organization's total activity. But, what is substantial? Get ready for a milestone in bureaucratic doubletalk: IRS Regulation 1.501(c)(3)(1)(c) provides that an organization will lose its tax-exempt status if "more than an insubstantial part of its activities is not in furtherance of an exempt purpose." So what is "substantial"? The IRS defines it as "more than insubstantial"! And I dare not ask how the IRS would define "insubstantial"; the answer would probably be "less than substantial"!

The regulation goes on to say, however, that in determining whether or not the activities are substantial, "all the surrounding facts and circumstances, including the articles and activities of the organization, are to be considered."

It is tempting to look to percentages of total activity as a measure of substantiality. The courts have referred to percentages from time to time, but have never expressly adopted a percentage rule as an absolute test. For one thing, we have to ask, percentage of what? Percentage of the total church budget? Percentage of the pastor's time? Percentage of office space allocated? Percentage of members or staff involved? Most likely the courts would look at all of these factors taken together.

From the case of *Seasongood v. Commissioner*, 227 F2d 907 (6th Cir. 1955), it appears that if the church's efforts to influence legislation constitute less than 5 percent of its total activity, the church is quite safe. If efforts to influence legislation constitute between 5 percent and 20 percent of the total activity, the case could go either way depending upon all of the facts and circumstances involved—and, to be quite candid, depending upon the inclination and prejudices of the IRS agent who handles the case. If efforts to influence legislation constitute more than 20 percent of the church's total activity, the church's tax-exempt status is in serious jeopardy.

At the time one applies for tax-exempt status, it is possible to make an election under 501(h) of the IRS code. This election effectively places the organization under a special rule whereby the question of whether your organization's legislation-influencing activities are "substantial" is determined by looking at the organization's gross expenditures. If less than 20 percent of the expenditures are directed toward influencing legislation, your organization meets the political test under 501(c)(3), provided all other criteria are met.

If you do not make the 501(h) election, the IRS uses a "totality of circumstances" test for determining whether or not your lobbying activity is "substantial."

If your organization is already tax-exempt under 501(c)(3), you can still make the election for future years, though, you cannot make it retroactively.

Influencing Elections

As we have seen, influencing legislation cannot be a substantial part of your total activity. Influencing elections, on the other hand, is forbidden entirely.

What's the difference? Simply put, working to defeat a bill to establish school-based clinics in the public schools is influencing legislation. Working to elect Jack Kemp as president of the United States is influencing elections.

But, what constitutes influencing elections? If Pat Robertson preaches or is introduced at your church, that might constitute influencing elections; but, if your church offers a candidates' forum at which all of the candidates are invited to appear, that probably is OK. If your church organizes a group to go door to door passing out literature for William Bennett, that is influencing an election. But, if your church conducts a nonpartisan voter registration drive, that probably is permissible. Obviously, a church could not give money to a political campaign or endorse a political candidate.

According to IRS Reg. 1.501(c)(3)-1(c)(iii), the term "candidates for public office means an individual who offers himself, or is proposed by others, as a contestant for an elective public office, whether such office is national, state or local." So long as the office is elective, it does not matter whether it is partisan (that is, the candidate runs under a party label, such as Democrat or Republican) nor nonpartisan (See Rev. Rul. 67-71, 1967-1 C.B. 125). Urging the mayor or governor to appoint a new police chief or judge would not constitute influencing elections. The same is true of urging the selection of a Supreme Court Justice, though it is possible that that might constitute influencing legislation since the Senate must confirm the nomination.

It appears the IRS is tightening up on candidate surveys. Various organizations, Right and Left, have surveyed candidates for public office on how they have voted or would vote on key issues of concern, and then distributed the results of the survey to their adherents. The IRS now appears to be saying that such surveys constitute influencing elections and could cause a church to lose its tax-exempt status. Such surveys are probably permissible provided the following guidelines are followed: (1) Only incumbent office-holders are surveyed, not their opponents; (2) The survey is not timed to an election; and, (3) The published survey does not comment on the results, indicating "A 'yes' vote on this issue is a good vote," etc. See Rev. Rul. 78-248, 1978-1C.B. 154; Rev. Rule. 80-282, 1980-2C.B. 178: G.C.M. 39441, November 7, 1985.

Other Observations

The above prohibitions affect the church as an organization, not necessarily the individuals involved therein. While the board of Christ the Redeemer Lutheran Church could not endorse a single candidate for the presidency, Pastor Erickson may do so as an individual and may indicate his credential as a pastor in doing so. Whether he may do so from the pulpit is uncertain. Attorney James F. Schoener of the Washington, D.C. Law Firm of Jenkins, Nystrom & Steriacm believes he may do so (letter from Schoener to Rev. D. James Kennedy, Coral Ridge Presbyterian Church, 17 April 1980). There are, however, indications that IRS officials may now disagree with that position.

If the church gives its membership list to a political campaign, that might constitute political activity. But if the candidate buys the list and if other candidates could also buy it, that would be ok. On the other hand, if the church directory is available to the members, then any individual member could give the directory to the campaign and that would not present a problem.

The church may not give money to a candidate, and may not give a substantial portion of its money to lobbying organizations. But, there is no problem with individuals doing so.

Some groups find it necessary to establish two corporations—one to conduct educational religious charitable and other tax-exempt activities and the other to engage in political activity. An avowedly political organization might set up an educational arm that qualifies for 501(c)(3) tax-exempt status, and channel its tax-exempt activities and contributions through that organization. A religious organization might set up a political arm that is not tax-exempt but is free to engage in political activity. Your church might consider following that course of action if you wish to direct a substantial portion of your activities to politics.

I emphasize in closing that the law in this area is fluid and changing. While this article does not constitute the giving of legal advice and should not be relied upon as an ironclad statement of the law, I hope it will be helpful to those who want to know what they can do politically without running afoul of the IRS.